AS GOES CALIFORNIA

My Mission to Rescue the Golden State and Save the Nation

LARRY ELDER

BOMBARDIER
BOOKS

Published by Bombardier Books
An Imprint of Post Hill Press
ISBN: 978-1-63758-600-6
ISBN (eBook): 978-1-63758-601-3

As Goes California:
My Mission to Rescue the Golden State and Save the Nation

Cover Design by Hampton Lamoureux

All people, locations, events, and situations are portrayed to the best of the author's memory. While all of the events described are true, many names and identifying details have been changed to protect the privacy of the people involved.

BOMBARDIER BOOKS

Post Hill PRESS

Post Hill Press
New York • Nashville
posthillpress.com

Published in the United States of America
1 2 3 4 5 6 7 8 9 10

CONTENTS

Foreword
BY CANDACE OWENS

"If I HAVE SEEN FURTHER, it is by standing on the shoulder of giants."

That quotation was written in a letter dated 1675, from Isaac Newton. It ranks as one of my favorite metaphors, as it so perfectly illustrates my own political contributions. If I have been able to contribute anything to the national conversation, let it be known that it is by the grace of those that came before me.

It has been said that for children, most lessons are caught rather than taught. The first giant I came across in life was undoubtedly my late grandfather, a man who led only by example. A man whose life and value system stood in stark contrast to the familial and cultural breakdown we witness so clearly in America today. He believed in secular abstinence, which kept him immersed in works of faith. He knew that happiness could only be found through the eternal source of God. In my adolescence, I resented those beliefs. Pleasure, as I had learned through public education and cultural conditioning, could also be derived from material things. Because like so many others, I was having my ideas engineered by a society on the brink of steep cultural decline. Having myself been immersed in far-left ideologies, I spent the early part of my twenties convinced that black people had to be Democrats and that police brutality and racial inequality would serve as inherent barriers to my success. So firmly committed was I to these philosophies that one would have had better luck moving a mountain than moving me away from them.

Larry Elder was the giant who moved that mountain.

There are few names as powerful in the black conservative movement as Larry Elder's. There are perhaps even fewer names in the current landscape of political intellectuals, and there are positively no names that have proven more crucial to my own awakening.

My introduction to Larry Elder can only be described as a secondhand, intellectual assault. I was aimlessly scrolling on Youtube one day, when I came across a clip of him speaking to show host Dave Rubin, regarding the topic of police brutality. Rubin (presenting a liberal perspective) quizzed Elder on the reasons as to why Elder would (as a black man) refuse to accept that black Americans were being ruthlessly murdered by racist white police officers. Elder rebutted him, instantly:

"Nine hundred sixty-five people were shot by cops last year. Four percent of them were white cops shooting unarmed blacks. In Chicago in 2011, twenty-one people were shot and killed by cops. In 2015 there were seven. In Chicago (which is about one-third black, one-third white, and one-third Hispanic) seventy percent of homicides are black on black—about forty per month, almost five hundred last year in Chicago and about seventy-five percent of them are unsolved.

"Where's the Black Lives Matter on that? The idea that a racist white cop shooting unarmed black people is a peril to black people is complete and total B.S.…The biggest burden that black people have in my opinion is the percentage of blacks—seventy-five percent of them—that are raised without fathers. And that has every other social negative consequence connected to it: crime, not being able to compete economically in the country, being more likely to be arrested, that's the number one problem facing the black community."

I remember my candid shock. The interview carried on in the same, academically-brutal fashion. Line after line of hard truth was fired by someone who could only be described as a statistical sharp-shooter. The end result was that Dave Rubin looked like an errant schoolchild, being scolded by a teacher for failing to complete his assigned readings. And although I was not physically present, I shared in Rubin's shame. I was embarrassed by how little I knew; how equally incapable I would have been to rebuff a single fact that had been introduced by Elder. It was for me a pivotal moment in understanding how the liberal establishment had taken a singularity and turned it into a non-existent whole. Larry swiftly and adeptly disassembled the mainstream, emotional arguments, which, as I discovered, couldn't stand up to scrutiny.

From that point onward, Elder became instrumental in rebalancing my understanding across a variety of topics, but it will always be the shattering of that first lie—the myth of police brutality—which opened a door for me that could never be closed. It was a "Big Bang" moment—an utter demolishment of a mainstream narrative—which springboarded me, as well as countless others, into our futures: a future unshackled from the victim narrative.

Which begs the question, who or what inspired Larry himself?

Elder's story of his father Randolph, which he has documented throughout his career, bears the hallmark of an American greatness known only to past generations. Elder describes his father as his personal hero. Randolph was a tremendously hard worker, who served as a janitor before one day becoming a successful café owner, which was his lifelong dream. His life offers a stunning rebuke of race-based narratives today. Just how is it that a man who experienced *actual* racism in an era when the hangover of generational racism was institutionalized, was able to find success? Just why is it that he did so without complaining and convicting the country as a whole? Just how was it that he was instead able to ignore the plenty of insults he received, adopting the mantra that "whatever doesn't kill you makes you stronger." Randolph would eventually retire after a long, successful entrepreneurial career. Just like my grandfather who would one day purchase the share-cropping farm that he grew up on, Elder's father, Randolph, was the embodiment of the American dream.

Looking backward to men like Randolph presents an opportunity to garner lessons for a struggling American society today:

Firstly, the need for a father figure. In a similar way that Christ talks of the prodigal son returning to the father, America needs to return fathers to their sons. The collapse of the nuclear family, a feature so dominant in the generation of Randolph and Robert, speaks volumes to the reason that black culture (and now all of American culture) has fallen into the gutter and continues to slide into the abyss of degeneracy. Value systems that are cultured in the loving embrace of father, mother, children, grandparents, can only be dreamed of when parts of this unit are picked off by the sirens of welfarism. Elder wrote about this in the foreword of my own book years ago, and here I am writing about it in the foreword of his. The issue hasn't been addressed, solved or even looked at by the progressive political parties that preach about fixing our broken society.

Secondly, the need for tough lessons. Ready to choose the easy path? Ready to amble along the road to destruction? Then adopt the black cultural narrative propounded by our society over the last sixty years. Be a victim, not a victor. Welfare slave, not a winner at work. Baby daddy, not a father figure, and so many more. These are what young Americans are being taught in the schools, in music, from both our political and Hollywood elite. Nowhere in this narrative can one find the truth: Life is tough. No one is entitled to an easy life and few are dealt a fair hand. But with the simple equation of faith, family and hard work, any person can bring to fruition an existence that gives back to the world.

The American dream is one that includes a meritocracy under which all can expect opportunity, but none should expect to be guaranteed success. Our country has been a philosophical experiment, comparatively greater than any other throughout human history. We came together as an experiment of freedom, but in recent years, we have been failing.

Because long gone are the tough lessons and wisdom of previous generations, instead replaced with undisciplined mantras which have brought forth laziness, tethered by a dark culture filled with narcissism and lies.

Indeed, this value system, or lack thereof, has now permeated our national identity. Look no further than California to see a third world nation on the verge of collapse, only supported by a federal life alert system of bailouts that keep the not-so-Golden state from its brink of collapse. Indeed the economic collapse and corruption is so endemic to California that the current Governor Gavin Newsom of California has been able to flagrantly flout his dictator-like laws and regulations without so much as batting an eyelid. Whereas a similar flouting of self-imposed Covid regulations in the United Kingdom effectively brought down a Prime Minister, Newsom still holds the office of Governor of a failing state. The woes of California have become so synonymous with socialism that Larry Elder chose the state as the location for his next battle—a battle well documented throughout this book.

Larry Elder for Governor of California. If there was one phrase I had not expected to hear when I was listening to that Rubin Report interview in 2017, it would have been that. But of course, no Elder move comes without meticulous research, planning and strategy, and no greater planning is required than to try and win a recall election. The historic recall election of 2003 that saw the displacement of Gray Davis with Arnold Schwarzenegger was a political earthquake that upturned what was possible in Sacramento politics. Elder hoped to recreate that magic in 2021, all over again.

And while I will leave it to Larry himself to detail that battle and the lessons learned from his experiences within a consequential, gubernatorial race, I will at first offer to you a quotation that will serve your interest throughout. It is one that many are familiar with, from a novel by G. Michael Hopf, "Hard times create strong men, strong men create good times, good times create weak men, and weak men create hard times."

There is no doubt that the good times of the last generation created many weak men, and that those weak men have allowed the hard times to fall upon us, particularly in Elder's home of California. No place is more synonymous with the historical easy-going life and sunshine paradise than that of California, yet no State in the Union bears the prophetic warning of what weak men can breed more aptly than the homeless-filled, drugged, illiberal dystopian nightmare that it has become.

Larry has spent his entire life fighting for and contributing to a better America. He inspired millions to choose a path that involves sacrifice and extreme diligence, but also enormous reward, pride, and achievement. For those willing to receive it, Larry has established the groundwork to truly comprehend the level of damage done by the welfare state. There is no person better versed in the government-sponsored destruction of the family unit and every societal ill which surrounds us today—a destruction conjured up in the halls of political establishments who bear little to no real experience to underpin their car-crash policies which have wreaked havoc upon American society up to the present day.

There is no doubt Elder has already indelibly left his mark on America, both directly and indirectly. His work and influence will bear fruit for generations.

If you thought that "Larry Elder for Governor of California" was something you weren't prepared to hear in 2021, buckle your seatbelt for another political tsunami to hit you in the pages of this book as Elder unveils his comeback plan from the West Coast to the White House.

Elder in name, Elder in wisdom. Mentor, political father figure and friend—thank you Larry for everything but not least of all revealing to me a very simple truth: that black people really don't have to be Democrats.

I will forever be humbled by the truth; that within the sphere of politics I am but a dwarf that has managed to catch a view, standing upon the shoulders of giants.

Ladies and gentlemen, I present to you, one of the giants.

Chapter 1

WHAT'S AT STAKE?

A FEW DAYS AFTER THE California gubernatorial recall election in 2021, I was sitting in a restaurant on the west side of Los Angeles. I had arrived early for dinner and, after checking my phone for emails, I just sat there looking around.

I think the two ladies at the next table felt sorry for me, sitting alone, and we started talking. Turns out they were eighty-five years old, had met in the second grade, and one of them had picked her favorite restaurant to celebrate her birthday. They told me they were Jewish. One called herself a "human rights activist," or something like that. The other said she had a psychotherapy practice.

About ten minutes into the conversation, one stopped herself in midsentence. "Wait a minute," she smiled and said. "I know you. You're that Larry Elder guy. You ran for governor."

"Guilty as charged," I smiled back.

"Guess who we voted for?" she asked.

"Well, you didn't vote for me."

"What makes you say that?"

"Let's see," I said. "You're both Jewish. We're in a restaurant on the westside of Los Angeles where Republicans are practically protected under the Endangered Species Act, and one of you is a 'human rights activist.' It doesn't take Colombo to put that together. You're both Democrats, and you most certainly did not vote for me. Am I right, or am I right?"

They laughed. "You're right."

"Of course I'm right. Bet you haven't voted for a Republican since the Titanic sank. But tell me, how do you feel about the crime here in Los Angeles?"

They both called it "outrageous," and one described in detail how a friend was recently a victim of one of those "follow out of the store" robberies, in which two thugs followed her friend out of a department store, tailed her friend to her high-end car, and followed her home. As she was waiting for her gate to open, they robbed her. Both verbally attacked Los Angeles district attorney George Gascon because, while the friend's suspects were not caught, the police told the friend, "Hopefully we will find them, but odds are they'll have criminal records, and wouldn't have been on the street in the first place if it weren't for our asshole DA."

"How do you feel about the homelessness?" I asked the ladies.

One called it "unconscionable." "It's not just a matter," she said, "of how bad it looks and that most of them are alcoholics, drug addicts, or mentally ill. It's not safe for the homeless population."

I replied that cops tell me that 100 percent of the female homeless have been raped, the only question is, how many times. One said that, just the other day, a homeless man living near her was found dead. "That's something," I said, "that happens at least five times a night on the streets, the parks, and under freeway overpasses here in Los Angeles County."

"I don't get it," one responded. "There's plenty of money in California, enough to house and treat them. Why aren't we doing this?"

We then turned to the quality of our public schools, which I call "government schools."

One lived in Los Angeles, the other in the San Fernando Valley, a more suburban part of the city.

"Do you have any friends who put their kids in government schools beyond elementary school?" I asked.

They looked at each other for a few seconds and admitted that, no, none of their Los Angeles-area friends placed their kids in government schools. Their friends, they said, put them in private or religious schools "at considerable cost."

We talked about the hundreds of thousands of Californians who, in the last couple of years, left the state for places such as Texas, Florida, Colorado, and Nevada. They both knew friends and coworkers who had done just that.

Because of their age, they said, they have been vaccinated, but didn't understand why California governor Gavin Newsom shut down the whole state, including schools, especially when "he was at that restaurant and wasn't even wearing a mask."

Our conversation continued for several minutes, at which point, my friend arrived. I introduced him to the ladies and recapped our conversation:

"For the last twenty minutes, these ladies and I practically completed each other's sentences about crime, homelessness, the pathetic state of public education, and how Gavin Newsom ignored science and shut down the state. Yet, they didn't vote for me. And I'll tell you why."

I smiled at the ladies and said: "Even though you agreed with me on every major campaign issue, you...just...couldn't... bring...yourself...to...pull...that...lever...for...a...a...Republican!"

They laughed. "Do you have any conservative friends?" I asked. They looked at each other for a moment, and admitted that they did not.

"When was the last time you had a conversation," I asked, "like the one we just had, with a Republican?"

"Well..." one said, "never." The other said, "Not in the last few—"

"Decades." I interrupted. We all laughed.

The human rights activist said, "What are you drinking?" By the end of our little encounter, they bought both of my drinks and picked up the tab for my lobster dinner.

"If we had known you were like this, we might've voted for you," they said.

"You'd be surprised," I said. "There are lots of us. We don't have horns. We don't have tails. We don't bite the heads off baby seals. You and I want the same things: for people to realize their God-given potential, right?"

I have these conversations all the time, and no wonder. When I ran for governor in 2021, many of the issues the people of California faced were the same as those troubling the rest of the country. Some were the result of an immediate failure of Democratic governance, such as the repressive COVID-19 lockdowns. But most had been percolating for decades: rising crime and homelessness, the failure of our K–12 public-school system, the absurd cost of housing, and, in California specifically, water shortages and uncontrollable wildfires.

But these problems were not the result of magical forces at work in the state. They were the direct consequences of man-made policies from Sacramento politicians and Demo-cratic governor Gavin Newsom. And, increasingly, these California policies are guides for Democrats nationwide.

Consider the following. Newsom ordered a more draconian COVID-19 lockdown than any other governor. He issued a dizzying number of directives, including the closure of most school campuses, a mask mandate, the vaccination of all state employees or regular testing, the mailing of ballots to all registered voters, and in-school student mask and vaccine mandates for most grades, public and private, as well as school staff vaccine mandates. All California counties were required to shut down restaurants, wineries, tasting rooms, movie theaters, family entertainment centers, zoos, museums, card rooms, and all bars.

Newsom signed a bill to restrict sentencing enhancements for certain crimes, including those committed by gang members. Gang members in California are disproportionately black and Hispanic, and to punish them severely would perpetuate "systemic racism." Never mind the disproportionate number of victims of gang crimes are black and Hispanic, and hardest hit by the combination of soft-on-crime policies and by the lie put forth by people like Newsom, who supported soft-on-crime DAs of San Francisco and Los Angeles County.

How hard hit? During the pandemic, Newsom, blaming COVID-19, granted the early release of eight thousand felons, including violent felons. What could possibly go wrong? The number of people shot in Los Angeles, year to year, was up 41 percent in 2020. Black and Hispanic neighborhoods were hit hardest.

Newsom signed a bill to establish a first-in-the-nation task force to study and issue recommendations for reparations. The task force recently issued its first report and proposed the implementation of "a comprehensive reparations scheme." How out of step is Newsom on reparations? In December 2021, the liberal Brookings Institute wrote: "Recent polling data documents Americans' general opposition to reparations in the form of financial payments to black Americans as compensation for slavery."

After the reversal of Roe v. Wade, Newsom proposed making California a "sanctuary state" for those seeking abortions. In signing a bill to provide "abortion rights" to those coming to California for abortions, Newsom said: "We will not aid, we will not abet in their efforts to be punitive, to fine and create fear for those that seek that support. We are proud to provide it—and we do."[1] In fact, California leads the way on abortion. For the last several years, Newsom has ramped up funding for abortion providers, offered tax breaks for companies seeking to move from states where abortion may be outlawed, and signed bills to protect abortion patients from privacy intrusions, insurance co-pays and threats, pressure or other attempts at "reproductive coercion." He also supports an amendment to the state's constitution to ensure "per-

1 Emma Gallegos, "Gov. Newsom Champions California as a Sanctuary for Those Seeking Abortion," EdSource.org, June 24, 2022, https://edsource.org/updates/gov-newsom-champions-california-as-a-sanctuary-for-those-seeking-abortion.

sonal reproductive liberty," an amendment that could permit third-trimester abortions.

These policies are popular with the far left, but most other people—Republicans and Democrats alike—think they go too far. It wasn't a surprise that in 2021 the effort to recall and replace Newsom produced 1.6 million valid voter signatures, one hundred thousand more than necessary to trigger the second gubernatorial recall election in California history. Nearly one-third of those who signed the recall petition voted for Newsom only two years earlier. Californians saw their Golden State irrevocably tarnished and felt that life here might never recover. For those who wanted to stand their ground and fight, this recall provided a historic chance to reset, to restore common sense, and end the attack on the middle and working class that caused a net loss of population for the first time in California's 170-year history. The recallers were a diverse group with one main thing in common: We love California.

When I entered the recall race, the polls suddenly showed the odds of recalling Governor Newsom within the margin of error of the 50 percent needed to recall him. The shock of these new polls scared Newsom. They scared Democrats nationwide. If deep-blue California could jettison a Democratic governor, who, just three years earlier, won by twenty points, this awakening could happen *anywhere.*

Although I was by far the most popular GOP person in the race, my candidacy did not get the endorsement from the California Republican Party. That's because my supporters and I represented an insurgency, a grassroots movement, a different kind of earthquake that shook the political establishment in California and nationwide. We exposed an ossified political structure that sweeps problems under the rug, like the state's long-term debt and pension obligations. The problems California legislators seemingly ignored give states like Tennessee, Texas, and Florida a competitive advantage, allowing them to poach our people, our businesses, our tax base, and, for a Republican politician, as I was for eight weeks—our votes.

In a frenzy of hyper partisanship and negativity, Newsom, a man of privilege whose father was a tax attorney for the oil-rich Getty family, fought off the recall like a cornered animal. He did not defend his record. He did not even try. Nor did his supporters inside or outside California do so. He survived the recall against him in California by shouting at every turn, "Stop the Republican takeover!" He provided no answer on rising crime. No answer on growing homelessness. No answer on the massive unfunded public sector pension liability. No answer on reversing the migration out of California. He won because he resorted to the only strategy that could win: convincing voters that a black candidate from the inner city whose father cleaned toilets was scarier than the prospect of reforming California. Why? The black candidate is a Republican who voted for...Donald Trump. What could be worse?

During my campaign, I never suggested that anyone should vote for or against me because I'm black. Others made much about my potentially becoming California's first black governor. I did not. As far as I'm concerned, after the election of Barack Obama, the nation's first black president, as to the first black this or that, everything else becomes pretty much anticlimactic.

But my candidacy posed a problem for the left-wing media and its obsession with identity politics. A black *Los Angeles Times* columnist, Erika Smith, called me "The black face of white supremacy" and that my candidacy "feels personal. Like an insult to blackness."[2] Another *Los Angeles Times* columnist, Latina Jean Guerrero called my views "white supremacist" on CNN.[3] Former Public Broadcasting Service (PBS), National Public Radio (NPR), and television commentator, Tavis Smiley, called me "anti-black."[4] Only in America can a black person become president and another be maligned as a "white supremacist.

The recall survival left Newsom with an opportunity to finish out his term and make major changes to his disastrous policies. And his survival gave hyperpartisan news media another chance to redeem their forsaken public trust. But it got me thinking about the big issues again—and my friends noticed. After my California race, I've been asked by friends and donors, what's next? What about the presidency? Well, it's under serious consideration.

---

2 Erica D. Smith, "Larry Elder Is the Black Face of White Supremacy. You've Been Warned," *Los Angeles Times*, August 20. 2021, https://www.latimes.com/california/story/2021-08-20/recall-candidate-larry-elder-is-a-threat-to-black-californians.

3 Joseph A. Wulfsohn, "CNN's Stelter Allows Guest to Call Larry Elder a 'White Supremacist' Unchallenged, Avoids Racist Attack on Him," FOX News, September 12, 2021, https://www.foxnews.com/media/cnn-brian-stelter-larry-elder.

4 Julia Wisk, Erika D. Smith, "Larry Elder Draws Fire for N-Word Comedy Clip," *Los Angeles Times*, August 20, 2021, https://www.latimes.com/california/story/2021-08-20/larry-elder-draws-fire-for-n-word-comedy-clip.

If I decide to run for president, I would not view it as my "going up against Trump" or any other Republican, whether it's Governor Ron DeSantis or former vice president Mike Pence. I would see it as making my own case on how to make the country better—school choice, getting rid of soft-on-crime DAs, energy independence, real border security, and stopping the pitting of people against people with this critical race theory nonsense and the bogus narrative of American cops being "systemically racist." I'm for getting government off the backs of people so they can keep as much of their hard-earned money as they can. I'm for fixing the appalling public-school system, especially in the inner cities where it does a disservice to the many black children who rely on it because they do not have a father in the home.

"What about racism?" I am still asked. "Would that hold you back?" Really? In 2023? Are we STILL having this discussion? After the election and re-election of Obama? In fact, I can say that I am also considering a run for the presidency for "race relations" because of what Obama could have and should have done for the eight years of his presidency.

Especially on these issues, I believe I am uniquely qualified to speak in a way that most of my Republican colleagues are not. For nearly thirty years, I have made the case that for black people in California—and the entire nation—the American dream is available to everyone. You only have to work for it. My mission to rescue California—and to warn the nation—only just began when I ran in the recall election. My supporters and I sparked a massive grassroots movement. It's time for voters, who refuse to abandon the state, to write a new script to restore not just the California dream but also to reaffirm the promise of America. When the Golden State shines, so does America.

We've got a country to save.

Chapter 2

WHAT MY PARENTS GAVE ME

I WAS BORN AND RAISED in Los Angeles, attended public school K–12, went to Brown University and the University of Michigan's law school. I worked for nearly three years at a large law firm in Cleveland, Ohio, after which I started and ran a Cleveland-based legal headhunting firm for fourteen years before selling it and moving back to LA, where I went into radio, television, and writing.

But ever since I was a little kid, politics has been my primary passion. When I was eight years old, my mom sat me down to watch the Democratic National Convention at the Cow Palace in San Francisco. Then we watched the Republican National Convention. We did it every four years. My two brothers couldn't care less about politics, but I was always interested in the big questions. In fifth grade, we were told to do a book report on a subject we found challenging. Most kids did theirs on butterflies, dogs, and cats. I did mine on communism. My parents always encouraged my love of politics, and when I ran against Newsom in 2021, my biggest regret is that neither my mom or dad were around to see it.

Although both of my parents inspired me, I especially looked up to my mother. Mom volunteered, taught Sunday school, cooked for friends and family, and made and mended dresses, shirts, socks and coats. She worked for the phone company, took up auto mechanics, and served as a seamstress coordinator for the opening and closing ceremonies of the 1984 Los Angeles Olympics. Our phone never stopped ringing with friends calling, seeking her advice, guidance or counsel, or offering an invitation to breakfast, lunch, dinner, a banquet, a barbecue, a wedding, a retirement party.

She performed the role of teacher, philosopher, and lawgiver. One time, my brother Kirk and I decided to "run away from home." Now, mind you, my parents' firm rule against crossing the street unaccompanied required us, as we fled from home, to stay within several hundred yards of the house—and on the same side of the street.

Who knew my dad could run? He caught us, and we started the long march home, where I knew that a severe whippin' awaited. Immediately, I took pre-emptive action. I started bawling right away.

"Boy, don't start that crying," said Dad, a tough World War II Marine vet. "Wait 'til we get home—I'll give you something to cry about." I tried apologizing. Nothing. I resorted to begging. We kept walking. I could practically feel the leather belt on my behind. Suddenly, a brilliant insight! I remembered the $2.75 in my piggy bank.

"Dad, if you don't whip me, I'll give you a dollar." He picked up the pace. "Two dollars?" Now we practically sprinted. "All right, Dad. Two dollars and seventy-five cents. All I have."

When we got home, I looked at Mom with watery but hopeful eyes. Surely, she would intervene, as she had done many times before, to, at the very least, lessen the punishment. But then my dad told her about the bribery attempt. "Son," my mother said to me, "you're on your own."

For her last several years, my mother appeared as a guest every Friday on my radio show. I called her the "Chief Justice of the Supreme Court," and she gave her commonsensical take on world affairs. Her solution to illegal aliens from Mexico? Invade Mexico, develop it, and turn it into the fifty-first state. She was kidding...I think.

For five minutes on Thursdays, my mom provided movie reviews. (The day before she died, she called me to suggest possibilities for her next movie.) She quickly became the most popular feature on the show. At the end of each segment, I always said on air, "I love you, Mom," to which she either said nothing or mumbled something like, "Your daddy sends his love." In the fifty-four years I knew my mother, I can count on one hand the times she said, "I love you."

After her passing, one of my listeners sent a note of condolence: "Being from the Midwest, I understand perfectly why she didn't verbalize her love for you on the air! We just don't do it that way, and we believe constantly repeating the phrase lessens its value."

The Friday before she passed, a caller from North Carolina paid her the ultimate compliment. Because of her warmth, down-to-earth nature, and politically incorrect, tell-it-like-it-is, Southern, down-home manner, he pronounced Viola Elder "America's mom."

When I was seven, she and I read out loud an illustrated book of all the presidents, from George Washington to the then-incumbent, Dwight Eisenhower. When we finished, she closed the book, tapped it, and said, "Larry, someday you could be in this book."

I never wanted to be in that book and was never interested in politics except as a critic and commentator. But I knew, given my mother's confidence, that I could reach any goal I chose. About my shot at being governor of California, she would have been over the moon. She would have spoken at my rallies, given interviews, and might well have made it more difficult for the media to caricature me as Darth Vader. She taught my brothers and me to stand up for ourselves, to hold our ground, and to refuse to compromise on principle. One of her granddaughters said, "She taught me how to be a woman." Well, my mom, aka the "chief justice"—along with my wonderful father—taught me how to be a man.

The lessons I received from my father were often tough. My dad was born in Athens, Georgia, in 1915 or thereabouts. His exact birth date is not known because he was born in a shack to an illiterate single mother who abandoned him when he was only thirteen. With no father to turn to, young Elder relied on himself. A black man-child, on his own in the Deep South, Randolph Elder made a living working various odd jobs. Eventually he saved up enough money to start his own taxicab company, but when he went to the local courthouse to apply for a business license, it turned out the judge happened to own a cab company, using black cab drivers, in the same black area of town where my dad wanted to operate. The judge refused his license, saying in open court, "Why should I give another nigger a license?"

So he became a Pullman porter, traveling on the railroads all around the country, and on a trip to California was astonished that a black man could walk in the *front* door of a restaurant and get served. In the South, he always carried little boxes of crackers and tins of tuna because, he said, you never knew how long it would be before you could get something to eat.

After the bombing of Pearl Harbor, he joined the Marine Corps, becoming a Montford Point Marine, the first black Marines to serve. He was stationed on the island of Guam, reached the rank of staff sergeant and was put in charge of cooking for the "colored" soldiers. In 2012, Congress belatedly awarded the twenty thousand Montford Point Marines a Congressional Gold Medal. My dad received his posthumously.

After the war, my dad returned home hoping to land a job as a short order cook in Chattanooga, Tennessee, where he met and married my mom. But he was rejected at every restaurant because the owners said, "We don't hire niggers."

So he moved to California, but still no restaurants would hire him, claiming that despite his years as a Marine cook he "lacked references." He even offered to work two weeks for free in place of the allegedly required "reference." There were no takers. So he went to an employment office, sat in a chair for a day and a half, and finally got a job working for Nabisco Bread as a janitor where his primary job was cleaning toilets. He worked a second full-time job at another bread company called Barbara Ann Bread, where he also cleaned toilets.

He went to night school three or four nights a week to get his GED. Though my mom stayed home until the youngest of my three brothers was in middle school, dad somehow managed to save enough money to start his own business, a small restaurant, in the Pico-Union area of Los Angeles, which remained open until he retired at age eighty-two. When he retired, his net worth was a little under a million dollars. My dad truly lived his belief in the power of hard work, and he was a lifelong Republican. About the other party, he always told my brothers and me this: "Democrats want to give you something for nothing. And when you try and get something for nothing, you almost always end up getting nothing for something."

Every time I achieved something my dad thought impressive, he'd say, "My goodness!" Among them—becoming an Ivy League-educated lawyer, becoming a nationally syndicated columnist; having two nationally syndicated television shows, becoming a nationally syndicated radio host, being a keynote speaker at the Reagan Library where my picture is displayed on a wall, having a small private dinner with Nancy Reagan, attending the intimate Ronald Reagan funeral in Simi Valley, appearing on *The Tonight Show* hosted by Jay Leno to discuss my *New York Times* bestseller *The Ten Things You Can't Say in America*, and appearing on the *Oprah Winfrey Show*.

Dad had already died when, in 2015, I produced a documentary called *Uncle Tom: An Oral History of the Black Conservative*, and received a star on the Hollywood Walk of Fame (the film scored a higher IMDb rating than the five 2020 Best Documentary film Academy Award nominees). He also died before I became a television host and producer of *The Larry Elder Show* for the *Epoch Times*. I bet he would have gotten a kick out of seeing me travel up and down California, doing nearly one hundred events in seven-and-a-half weeks in my campaign for governor.

More than anything, both of my parents primed me to understand the world as a place where the path of your life is determined primarily by your own decisions—and not by your racial background. From when I was ten until I was fifteen, I worked in my father's restaurant. The clientele was about a third black, a third white, and a third Hispanic. All the white people I ever ran into were basically nice, decent people. I didn't grow up influenced by the resentments so many black people have today. In fact, I was often the one least concerned about race!

I remember one summer I was at a Cub Scouts camp in Yucaipa, along with hundreds of other boys. When I stood up on a hill and looked down on all the people, I could see only a handful of black dots. Almost everyone else was white. My cabin was almost all white. After a few days of getting to know each other, one of the guys called me a "nigger." I don't know why he did it. I don't remember how I replied. But I do remember that I had to literally restrain the other guys from beating the crap out of this guy. They were angrier than I was.

And when I look back on my childhood, I know why: many white people still feel really, really, really guilty about slavery and Jim Crow and the way that black people were treated in this country up until the middle of the twentieth century. And many of black people do the opposite, nursing old hatreds for crimes they never personally experienced.

But when I look back on my parents, I realize why I never had this tendency. Through his example, my father taught me never to construe the worst possible reason for an incident.

Instead, his advice encouraged his kids to be self-reliant, so we wouldn't have to endure what he went through. He was always telling us that hard work wins. "You get out of life what you put into it," he said. "You cannot control the outcome, but you are 100 percent in control of the effort. Before you moan and groan about what somebody did to you or said to you, go to the nearest mirror, look at it and ask yourself, 'What can I do to change the outcome?'" And my dad always said to my brothers and me, "No matter how hard you work, how good you are, sooner or later bad things are going to happen to you."

When my older brother, on Friday the thirteenth in 2019, suddenly died of a heart attack, I thought back on the full life he had lived. Kirk was a retired supervisor at an oil refinery. We were extremely close. He started coming on my radio show about four years beforehand, reluctantly at first. We'd discuss politics, culture, and sports. A registered Democrat, he and I often disagreed. Yet, week after week, I received letters from listeners who called him their "favorite Democrat." Kirk always showed respect for Republicans—and, yes, even Trump supporters—with whom he differed on policy but whose motives he never maligned.

Kirk had four children, two sons and two daughters, and loved—truly *loved*—being a father. He had no enemies. Everyone liked him. On the radio, he often talked about his "favorite watering hole" and his discussions, mostly sports, with its "regulars." After he died, I asked his wife Tresta for the name and location of that bar. I went there. I walked up to some men sitting at the bar, asked if they knew Kirk and introduced myself as his brother. Within minutes, I was surrounded by people who offered their condolences and told story after story about their fun battles with Kirk over his support for the Los Angeles Raiders. They told me of his kindness and generosity and how he bought birthday and Christmas presents for the bar staff.

Growing up, I had friends who had older brothers and complained that they bullied them. Kirk, though big and strong, never bullied my younger brother Dennis and me, something I didn't truly appreciate until I was much older. Because of his gentleness, I thought of him as soft—until he beat the crap out of the neighborhood bully who'd started a fight. Who knew Kirk had that in him? About the vanquished tough guy, my mother said, "He picked on the wrong kid."

Kirk dragged my little brother and me to every Elvis Presley movie, including the bad ones, and a lot were bad. Because Kirk was the oldest, my parents gave him the movie and popcorn money along with permission to choose the movie. So off to the latest Elvis movie we went. Kirk embraced Muhammad Ali, then called Cassius Clay. Our boxing-savvy father dismissed the "Louisville Lip" as an upstart loudmouth and predicted Clay's "destruction" in the upcoming fight with the heavyweight champ, the seemingly invincible Sonny Liston. Liston lost. Kirk crowed.

We played Little League hardball, but on opposing teams. A pitcher, Kirk mowed me down in our little backyard and in the streets where we played. But in the two times our Little League teams squared off with him pitching, I managed to hit two triples, two doubles and three singles. He denied "easing up" on me, but to this day I wonder.

A few years before my father died, I visited Dad, finding him in the garage "throwing out old stuff." Thank goodness I stopped Dad before he threw out "some old letter" he'd written. Dad, for whatever reason, felt he would die at age thirty-six. So he wrote Kirk, then two years old, this letter of advice and guidance that even now I turn back toward, excellent advice from any father to a son:

> May 4, 1951
>
> Kirk, my Son, you are now starting out in life—a life that Mother and I cannot live for you.
>
> So as you journey through life, remember it's yours, so make it a good one. Always try to cheer up the other fellow.
>
> Learn to think straight, analyze things, be sure you have all the facts before concluding and always spend less than you earn.
>
> Make friends, work hard and play hard. Most important of all, remember this: The best of friends wear out if you use them.
>
> This may sound silly, Son, but no matter where you are on the 29th of September [Kirk's birthday], see that Mother gets a little gift, if possible, along with a big kiss and a broad smile.
>
> When you are out on your own, listen and take advice but do your own thinking and concluding,

set up a reasonable goal and then be determined to reach it. You can and will. It's up to you, Son.

Your Father,
Randolph Elder

Chapter 3

ANOTHER ROUTINE SPECTACULAR PLAY

YOU COULD SAY MY CAREER in political commentary began almost by accident. I was living in Cleveland and running a successful legal headhunting firm. Of course, I was naturally interested in politics and often sent op-eds to the *Cleveland Plain-Dealer*, which was then one of the most read papers in the state. They were all turned down until I sent in one in the late '80s where I argued that racism was not the issue it once was in America. In fact, I said, in America, the sky was the limit for black people. The next morning, I got a phone call from a talk radio producer who'd read my article. He invited me on his host's show.

I had never really listened to talk radio. I lived in downtown Cleveland, walked to work and never had the experience, as many do, of listening to talk radio in the car to and from work. My mom, however, loved talk radio and always had it on at home as I was growing up. KABC in Los Angeles was the first 24/7 talk radio station in the world; it came on air around 1965.

Cleveland is about 50 percent black, and virtually all the callers were blacks. Every single one of them blasted me for my "Pollyannish" article on "race." Several called me an Uncle Tom. One denounced me as a bootlicking Uncle Tom. Another called me a bug-eyed bootlicking Uncle Tom. Another called me a bug-eyed, bootlicking, foot-shuffling Uncle Tom. Oreo. Coconut. One even said I was the anti-Christ.

On the drive back to my office I swore I'd never do that again. But the station manager called and said, "You were amazing. You are funny. You defended difficult positions without losing your sense of humor or your temper. Have you ever thought about doing talk radio?" He offered me a one-week tryout because one of his hosts was set to go on vacation. "No," I said. He asked why. "I don't like yelling. I don't like being yelled at." He paused, then asked, "Are you married?" At the time I was. He said, "Do me a favor and go home tonight and ask your wife about this." I said that I would. "But I won't change my mind," I warned him.

My wife Cindy asked what I knew about talk radio. I said, "Nothing, other than it seems shallow, glib, and stupid." She said, "It is. You'd be good at it." We laughed and I said, "Okay, let me give it a try."

I sat in for that whole week. I thoroughly enjoyed it and made a twenty-minute sample cassette tape, which I sent to three stations in Los Angeles: KABC, KFI, and a black radio station, KGFJ. Then I called the stations. "My name is Larry Elder. I sent you a tape." The response? "You sent a tape to who? For what? I can't find it. Send it again." No doubt most dropped it in the "circular file" for unsolicited packages. I sent another to each place. I followed up with more calls. It was always the same thing. I know it got dropped in the trash can. And I didn't think much more about it until I appeared on Dennis Prager's radio show in 1992.

Up to that point, media was nowhere near my primary career. But I made regular appearances on Cleveland morning shows where I would comment on the news from a lawyer's perspective. One morning I walked into the studio, and there was Dennis, who happened to be in town and was guest hosting that day. We did a few segments together, and during one of the breaks, I overheard someone ask him when he was going back to LA.

"LA?" I said, and told him how I grew up there. And on the spot, he invited me to come on his show the next time I was in town. When I told my mother about the conversation, she informed me that he had paid me a high compliment, since Dennis "rarely has guests". So the next time I was in town, I made sure to call him.

When I did appear on his show, we discussed my conservative views and how I arrived at them. Afterward, Dennis effusively praised my performance, saying I had fired off the funniest line he'd ever heard on radio. On his show, I had harshly criticized Jesse Jackson, Al Sharpton, and Louis Farrakhan. All three then—as they are now—were considered black leaders, but what have they ever preached but grievance? (I find it telling that in the four decades since, not a single one has ever agreed to appear on my show.) A black man called and angrily said, "Dennis, where'd you get this guy talking all this smack about Sharpton and Farrakhan and Jesse Jackson?" Dennis let me answer. "Well, sir, I was standing on the corner of Florence and Denker holding up a sign that said: 'Will speak negatively about black leaders for food.' Dennis pulled over, and that's why I'm here." Dennis laughed so hard he told his engineer to go to a commercial break.

Afterward, I told him the story about my sending a sample tape to LA radio stations, including his, and that nobody cared. Dennis promised to get management to listen to the tape and said he would try to get me an audition at KABC.

I flew back to Cleveland and when I walked into my office Monday morning, I received a call from KABC Station Manager George Green. "Heard you on the Prager show. Have you ever thought about doing talk radio?" He asked me to fly back to LA and said he'd put me on the air for a couple of days. I returned and did the first of two three-hour shows. After the first night, Green offered me a job. He said, "Do your next show. Have fun, and don't speak so damn quickly."

I've been on the radio ever since.

Now, over the years, I have basically addressed every live political and cultural issue on my shows or in my weekly column, which I have written since the Clinton presidency. And in the beginning, it was a real shock for most people—a black conservative constantly on the air not bowing to the established norms of political commentary. There were few black conservatives in the limelight then, and the ones doing some of the best work—the economist Thomas Sowell is a great example—rarely got the credit they deserved.

In the first year, I received fierce backlash from some self-appointed local activists, who were on fire about my suggestions that hard work and perseverance in the workforce were the natural next steps for blacks after civil rights. A group called Talking Drum Community Forum Group sent incessant letters to my sponsors claiming that I demeaned black people and spouted racism. Many of my advertisers pulled their support and I had to travel to their headquarters in person to win it back. I even met with some of the activists, but it was useless. They didn't even listen to the show: They just wanted me off the air.

Eventually I became more established, and that particular trouble died down. One day I got a phone call from a woman named Sister Malik. She said she was a member of one of these groups and that she wanted to meet me somewhere. A friend who's a cop in Inglewood agreed to go along with me in case something went south. So, we went down to an Arby's and he sat in a booth in the corner while I waited for Sister Malik. When she came in, she was wearing an African headdress: She looked the part.

But when we sat down, she surprised me by bursting into tears.

"I'm so sorry," she said. "I finally listened to your show, and I see now. All you're saying is work hard, don't blame other people, invest in yourself. What in the world is so controversial about that?"

She apologized, and I accepted. It was a seminal moment.

I started having moments like these frequently. One time I was walking down the street in LA when I had been on the air for about three months. I was still dealing with the activists and was getting all sorts of crap from black people generally. These two brothers leaning on a wall saw me on the way to a restaurant near my office. One yelled at me.

"Hey, come over here!"

I thought, if the guy was going to shoot me, he would have done it already. So I walked over. What did I have to lose?

"I know who you are. I wouldn't listen to your show for five weeks. I just couldn't stand you," he said. "But now I see what you are you doing. You're telling us to get off our ass and take advantage of the advantages of America. Keep doing what you're doing."

I nodded.

"You're like castor oil. It don't taste good going down, but it's good for you," he said. "I got your back, bro."

But conversations like this are mostly the exception. My message, which to me seems like commonsense, is highly offensive to those whose established order it challenges. And over the years, I've noticed a few areas, especially in questions of race, where even though the truth seems so obvious, so many people can't—or refuse to––see it.

The biggest one is probably the O. J. Simpson trial, where anyone with working eyes could see that he was guilty. But there was a subtext to the trial that very few white people understood until the whole thing blew up. Most white people had, and still have, no idea how resentful and angry black people are. And the trial exposed that side of the black community to many white people for the first time. I said that during an interview at the time on *60 Minutes* and it was considered shocking. Because after all, the evidence of O. J.'s guilt was all there: hair evidence, blood evidence, fiber evidence, blood in the car, blood on the sock. He had beaten Nicole Brown before. Everything was there.

But I noticed a funny thing was happening. Even though everyone knew O. J. did it, black people were willing to turn a blind eye to the evidence. During that *60 Minutes* segment, Morley Safer, who was interviewing me, noted that he worked with a black staffer who was extremely bright, but had an O. J. blind spot. It got to the point, he said, that he couldn't even talk about O. J. because she was convinced that the LAPD had set him up—even though the police chief at the time was black.

I had a Chilean friend in the fashion business who said something similar. She and her coworkers watched the trial whenever it was shown on the news and they were all convinced that O. J. did it. But when the verdict dropped, and he was pronounced not guilty, a black kid, who the entire time had said that O. J. did it, leapt up and cheered. He caught himself, but not before everyone in the office noticed.

There was an incredible piece in *The New Republic* after the trial that exposed how much blacks bought into the conspiracy theory that O. J. was framed by racist cops. A teacher in New Jersey noted that of the one hundred or so children he taught, all had a different theory exonerating O. J. One of them said Kato Kaelin did it. Another said A. C. Collins. Another blamed the dog. Not a single one of the black women had any sympathy at all for Nicole. They were angry at her for taking O. J. away from his first wife, Marguerite, who was black. And anytime a student said anything at all to the contrary, the other students pounded on him until he reverted to the position that O. J. was innocent.

To me, that was just scary—a massive refusal to use simple common sense. But since the verdict was delivered in

1995, it has begun to make more sense. The majority of blacks now say that they believe O. J. did, in fact, do it. Ignoring the evidence was not a matter of stupidity. It was intentional, a revenge play. Even members of the jury have admitted it. In a recent documentary, Carrie Best, one of the women on the jury, said that 90 percent of the jurors decided to acquit O. J. as "payback" for what had happened to Rodney King, whose videotaped beating by white cops unleashed a massively destructive six-day riot in Los Angeles.[5] When the documentarian asked Carrie Best if she thought that was right, she just threw up her hands.

Only a year later, *USA Today* published a story claiming that a spate of black-church burnings highlighted a supposed "racial divide" in America. I was still pretty new at KABC, and the station asked me to cut a public service announcement to raise money to restore these black churches and deter racist whites from burning them down. I thought about it for a minute, and then said, "No, I don't believe this is really happening." A black woman working in community relations was furious with me.

"Larry, this is why black people hate your guts," she said.

I didn't care.

"Where's the evidence?" I said. "How does this story make any sense? All of a sudden, did some white racist say, 'Hey, I got an idea. Let's go burn black churches.' It doesn't add up."

When the dust settled, the numbers proved me right. More white churches were burning than black ones and more

5 Tim Molloy, "OJ Simpson Juror: Not-Guilty Verdict Was 'Payback' for Rodney King," *The Wrap*, June 15, 2016, https://www.thewrap.com/oj-simpson-juror-not-guilty-verdict-was-payback-for-rodney-king.

mosques and more synagogues too. Only a handful of these churches that were burned by white people were, in fact, burned as a result of somebody's race. Many incidents weren't even arson. The story was massive—and may have provoked actual racial tension—but it was all *USA Today*'s doing.

This incident and the O. J. Simpson case proved a point that I feel I have to make all the time. Once the supply of racism gets low, it becomes necessary to invent new sources.

In 1998, at a fifteen-hundred-seat theater in Leimert Park in South Central, I debated Steve Cokely, a then-aide to Chicago mayor Harold Washington, on the question "Is Hollywood racist?" People lined the street to get in. At first, the debate was to be held at the Masonic Temple in LA, but so many people wanted to attend, the debate was moved to a much larger former movie house. All but maybe five people in the standing-room-only crowd came to jeer me and to cheer Cokely, no matter how stupid the points he made. And there were many.

I argued facts. He argued emotion, conspiracy theories about "racist" Hollywood and secret antiblack meetings held behind closed doors. He talked about the systemic racism that supposedly still holds blacks back. I brought up the *Time*/CNN study that asked black teens if racism was a factor in their own personal lives. Eighty-nine percent said racism was a "small" or "no" problem in their own lives. I pointed out that the Screen Actors Guild, in 1996, found that 12 percent of acting jobs went to blacks, matching the percentage of blacks in America. The Directors Guild in 1995 said 3.9 percent of directing jobs went to black directors, but the next year it grew to 5.2 percent, a substantial increase. I showed a cover of

Ebony magazine with the headline: "Oprah, Debbie, Whitney, Tracey, Sparkle in the Year of the Black Woman Producer."

"Hollywood is not racist," I said. "Hollywood is rough, it is tough, and if you are unprepared to struggle, if you are unprepared to get rejection, then you should perhaps consider selling shoes. It is a tough, competitive business. Don't come unless you're willing to work hard, and you're willing to persevere and accept rejection." Many try, few get in, no matter their race.

Cokely called me a "victim." He talked about the demeaning and stereotypical black roles in movies from the 1930s. I responded, "It is now 1998." I said despite these demeaning roles, blacks have greater self-esteem than do whites. So, if Hollywood's intent was to damage the black psyche, I said, it hasn't worked.

The trend of inventing new sources of racism has become all the more common since the tame days of the '90s. Likely the most egregious fake hate crime of the past few years is that of television actor Jussie Smollett who, in January 2019, claimed two white men in "Make America Great Again" ball caps attacked him on the street at 2 a.m. in subzero weather, doused him with bleach, and put a noose around his neck. In early December 2021, a twelve-person jury found the former *Empire* actor guilty of five counts of disorderly conduct for making false reports to police. The "attackers" testified at the trial that Smollett hired them to stage the assault. The City of Chicago sued Smollett to recover more than $130,000 spent investigating his hoax. Smollett was sentenced to one hundred and fifty days in jail, thirty months of probation, and a fine of $25,000 and ordered to pay more than $120,000 in restitution to the city of Chicago.

Even Joe Biden fakes political hate crimes. On Martin Luther King Jr. Day in 2022, Biden called state laws requiring voter ID and the attempt to ban mass mailing of absentee ballots an "assault on our freedom to vote." He said, a little bizarrely, "What they're doing is worse than Jim Crow. It's Jim Eagle."[6] Never mind that black voters support voter ID, with some polls finding black support at nearly 80 percent. Calling for greater election security is somehow deemed racist.

Commentator Candace Owens, testifying before Congress, said that although white supremacists exist, their numbers are so minimal that white supremacy wouldn't make her list of the greatest problems faced by black Americans. She also noted that Democrats step up race-dividing accusations every four years, just in time for the next presidential election.

A great example is the case of Michael Brown, who was shot to death in 2014 by a white cop in Ferguson, Missouri. Brown was not exactly an innocent victim. He had troubles in his past and was caught on video violently assaulting someone shortly before the fatal confrontation. Even though the law officer who shot him did so in self-defense, the cry that went up around the country was that he had tried to surrender, saying, "Hands up, don't shoot." This turned out not to be true, but before the facts could be determined, Ferguson was burn-

---

6 Andrew Solender, "'Makes Jim Crow Look Like Jim Eagle': Biden Slams 'Despicable' GOP Voting Restrictions," *Forbes*, March 25, 2021, https://www.forbes.com/sites/andrewsolender/2021/03/25/makes-jim-crow-look-like-jim-eagle-biden-slams-despicable-gop-voting-restrictions.

ing and this false story was widely broadcast by the media, sparking similar unrest across the land.

The same is true of George Floyd. He had a record. He may have had an earlier clash with the officer who arrested him, when they both worked as bouncers at a club. The police came after him when a store clerk suspected that Floyd gave him a counterfeit twenty-dollar bill. Does anyone deserve to die over twenty dollars? Of course not. But were the riots that happened all over the country protesting the situation warranted? Floyd's dying words, "I can't breathe," became a rallying cry with even more impact than "Hands up, don't shoot."

In the trial of officer Derek Chauvin, the lead prosecutor--who happened to be black--stressed in his opening argument that the Minneapolis Police Department was not on trial. Nor, he said, were police officers, as a whole, on trial. And there was no evidence, however criminal Chauvin's behavior may have been, that the officer's actions were undertaken because Floyd was black. There were four officers on the scene. Two, including Chauvin, were white. One was a Hmong-American and the other, Alex Kueng, has a Nigerian father. After Kueng's arrest, his mother said, "That's part of the reason why he wanted to become a police officer—and a black police officer on top of it—is to bridge that gap in the community, change the narrative between the officers and the black community."[7] None of these facts mattered though, because by the time the

7 Kim Barker, "The Black Officer Who Detained George Floyd Had Pledged to Fix the Police," *New York Times* June 27, 2020, https://www.nytimes.com/2020/06/27/us/minneapolis-police-officer-kueng.html?searchResultPosition=1.

trial rolled around, the narrative was set and people had made up their minds.

Now, pointing out that most racial discrimination is played up for political ends has won me more enemies than friends, especially in California, where it is taken as gospel that racism is the most prevalent issue in the country right now. I've invited Jesse Jackson, Al Sharpton, and Louis Farrakhan to debate me on a regular basis for going on thirty years now. It's got to the point that they don't even call back because the answer is always no. I once ran into Jackson, went up, and asked him to come on my show. He grunted, "I'll get back to you." Never did.

You might think that at least "black leaders" worried about Los Angeles would come on my show and discuss the pressing issues. But no. I can't even count the number of times I've invited Los Angeles County Congresswoman Maxine Waters to come on my show. She always refuses. She once told feminist attorney Gloria Allred, then my fellow KABC talk show host, "I refuse to go on shows like Elder's. He's an entertainer. You, Gloria, are a serious journalist. I don't waste my time with entertainers."

I suppose she's entitled to that opinion, but I have to wonder why, when I was introduced to her in the Capitol building a few years later, she turned tail as fast as she could.

The congressman who introduced us, David Dreier, was shocked.

"You have no idea what a villain I am in the minds of people like this on the Left," I said. "She hates me more than almost anybody because I can knock down her argument—that we're victims and that America is wrecked by systemic racism and white people. To her, I'm a far bigger villain than a white Republican could ever be."

But it's odd that politicians like Waters spout these beliefs when they seem to know so little about the actual problems that their constituents face. Waters represents California's forty-third congressional district that encompasses cities such as Inglewood, Hawthorne, Gardena, and Torrance. Her constituents are 19.4 percent white, 21 percent black, 13.5 percent Asian, 1.6 percent Native American, and 47.5 percent Hispanic. It's hard to tell what she's doing for all these people. The schools are worse. The inner city is worse. Crime is higher. Familial breakdown is worse. Maybe it's time to take a look in the mirror and ask, "What am I doing wrong?"

But it's always easier to blame other people.

Though sometimes I wonder if the Maxine Waters of the world simply don't care about their constituents. House affordability is an instructive issue here. Maybe she won't come on my show because she fears that I might ask her about the 6,081-square-foot home, featuring eight bedrooms and five baths that she and her husband bought in 2004 in tony Hancock Park, now worth some $5 million. Waters has been serving in the House since 1991. Affordability is clearly not much of an issue for her.

In fact, "black leaders" who actually engage with reality are a rarity, and more often than not they go completely unappreciated. I was a teenager when I first saw the economist Thomas Sowell interviewed by William F. Buckley on his *Firing Line* television show. Fast forward years later. C-SPAN broadcast all four hours of my live radio show. I received a letter from Sowell congratulating me on my performance and complimenting me on the mastery of the issues I discussed that day. "Dear Larry, my wife and I watched the entire four hours. You were amazing. You're articulate. You were on top of the issues. I just want to say, splendid job."

For me, that was like getting a letter of approval from Elvis.

I've had the privilege of knowing Sowell for more than twenty-five years. I attended his eightieth birthday party, and another time he invited me to spend a weekend. More recently, he wrote to applaud my TV performance in an interview. He wrote, "As a sportswriter wrote about Willie Mays, 'Another routine spectacular play.'"

But as great as Sowell is, he gets almost no credit outside of right-leaning circles. The same is true of his good friend, the late fellow economist Walter Williams, and Supreme Court Justice Clarence Thomas. Every year, the black monthly magazine *Ebony* lists its "Power 100," defined as those "who lead, inspire and demonstrate through their individual talents, "the very best in black America." Each year Thomas is conspicuously absent. Apparently, as a sitting black justice on the Supreme Court of the United States, Thomas does not "lead, inspire and demonstrate...the very best in black America."

As for Sowell, he's only an economist and writer whom playwright David Mamet once called "our greatest contemporary philosopher." Sowell, who never knew his father, was raised by a great-aunt and her two grown daughters in Harlem, where he was the first in his family to make it past the sixth grade. He left home at seventeen, served as a marine in the Korean War, graduated magna cum laude from Harvard, and earned a master's degree at Columbia University the next year, followed by a PhD in economics at the University of Chicago. Even *Forbes* magazine has noted that it's a "scandal" that he has not been awarded the Nobel Prize. "No one alive has turned out so many insightful, richly researched books," the magazine wrote in 2015.[8] Yet because his ideas don't conform with the liberal narrative on black underachievement, many blacks have never heard of him.

The same is true of Williams. Raised by a single mother in Philadelphia's Richard Allen housing projects, he served as a private in the Army before earning a bachelor's degree at a state university, followed by a master's and a PhD in economics at UCLA. Williams wrote a dozen books on economics and race, including the inspirational *Up from the Projects: An Autobiography*, and was the subject of a documentary film before his death.

The exclusion of people like Thomas, Sowell, and Williams from the canon of great black Americans explains why there's no serious discussion in the black community about government dependency, school choice, and the damage done by high taxes, excessive regulation, and laws like minimum wage. And when I decided to run for governor, I found that the blackout extended to any black person who dares to challenge the media and Democratic party's narrative.

But speaking up is necessary. I am often reminded of this, especially when I'm out meeting people and giving speeches around California.

---

8 Steve Forbes, "Turning the Page on 2015," *Forbes*, November 4, 2015, https://www.forbes.com/sites/steveforbes/2015/11/04/turning-the-page-on-2015/.

A few years ago, I was speaking at a Republican club where almost everyone was white. The wait staff, on the other hand, was mostly black. This isn't uncommon, and usually they'll stop and listen to me. Afterward, I'll go and talk to them. The feedback is often positive.

Now this one time, as I was speaking, I noticed a huge black guy on staff standing in the back with his arms folded over his chest. He was not smiling. I maintained eye contact with him the entire time. Afterward, he came up to me.

Uh-oh, this could go south, I thought.

But what he said surprised me.

"I used to think that I was well-informed," he said. "But I had no idea that eighty-five percent of black eighth graders are not math or reading proficient. I had no idea that half of them were not even at basic proficiency in reading. I had no idea that seventy percent of black kids come into the world without a father in the home."

He kept repeating, "I had no idea. I had no idea. I had no idea."

"I'm mad at myself for being so ignorant," he said. "Thank you so much for opening my eyes." Then he walked away.

It's in those moments especially where I feel like my career has been worthwhile.

Chapter 4

CALIFORNIA'S LONG SLIDE DOWNHILL

ANYONE WHO'S LIVED IN CALIFORNIA as long as I have knows that the state has been sliding downhill for decades now. A recent study by the Cato Institute, the libertarian think tank, ranked California forty-eighth out of the fifty states in personal and economic freedom. The study also examines fiscal policy and regulatory policy.

For the first time, California's population decreased in 2020, resulting in the loss of a congressional seat. In the third quarter of 2021, one hundred and fifty thousand more people on average left the state versus sixty thousand net departures in the first quarter of last year. California's net loss of one-way U-Haul trucks grew worse from 2020 compared to the same time in 2021, the year of the recall.

It could have been worse. In 2020, U-Haul said it "ran out of inventory to meet customer demand for outbound equipment."[9] People depleted the stock of available vehicles—and had to wait to leave.

What does this mean? What does this tell us? U-Haul says: "While U-Haul migration trends do not correlate directly to population or economic growth, the U-Haul Growth Index is an effective gauge of how well cities are both attracting and maintaining residents."

Who wants to move to the Golden State these days? Between March 2020 and September 2021, there has been a 38 percent decrease in new arrivals. California has fifty-eight counties, and new arrivals fell in every single one.

Republican governors run Texas and Florida. They support pro-business and pro-labor policies, which translate to a lower cost of living compared to California. Florida and Texas have no state income tax, which means more money in the pockets of families. What's not to like, especially for those dealing with rising crime and homelessness? State taxes and regulations, as well as the lack of school choice are literally exporting good parents, who seek to raise their children in a healthy environment, to states like Texas and Florida.

It's much the same in any major Democratic city. Take Chicago, Barack Obama's adopted hometown. A Democratic stronghold for decades, Chicago weekend murder numbers rival those of a shooter video game. Want justice in the "City of the Big Shoulders?" Good luck! Some six hundred to seven hundred homicides every year go unsolved.

---

9 Media Relations, "U-Haul Ranks TEXAS the No. 1 Growth State of 2022," January 3, 2023, MyUHaulstory.com, https://myuhaulstory.com/2023/01/03/uhaul-ranks-texas-1-growth-state-of-2022/

Once a long-time Democrat-run major city goes bad, can it redeem itself? New York City murders declined 66 percent between 1993 and 2001. It saw a 72 percent decline in shootings, a 56 percent decline in the FBI Crime Index, a 45.7 percent decline in rapes, a 67.2 percent decline in robberies, a 39.6 percent decline in aggravated assault, a 68.2 percent decline in burglaries, a 43 percent decline in larceny, and a 73.3 percent decline in motor vehicle theft.

What was the secret? Republican mayor Rudy Giuliani and the NYPD followed a criminal justice policy known as "broken windows," which punished minor crimes like turnstile jumping based on the philosophy that "small time crooks" often go on to commit bigger crimes.

Contrast Giuliani's New York City to that under Bill DeBlasio.

Soft-on-crime district attorneys like LA County's George Gascon believe in get-out-of-jail-free policies like cashless bail and never prosecuting "juvenile" offenders as adults, no matter how heinous their crime. In Los Angeles, crime has skyrocketed. Those hurt most are the very black and brown people whom lefties like Gascon and Newsom—who appointed Gascon as DA of San Francisco County—claim to care about. Someone should alert Representative Maxine Waters. Maybe she'll finally discuss the mess on my radio show, after declining my many invitations to do so.

In late May 2020, Governor Gavin Newsom, after two days of riots sparked by the death in Minneapolis of George Floyd, declared a state of emergency in Los Angeles County and City, and activated the National Guard to assist police. The governor's action came at the request of Los Angeles mayor Eric Garcetti after he widened a mandatory curfew on the entire city. The Metro suspended all transit and the city in some areas resembled a war zone. Looters robbed and vandalized high-end shops at upscale The Grove shopping center in the Fairfax district. Looting occurred on Fairfax and Melrose Avenues, where thieves ransacked stores. Local news viewers watched in horror as looters broke into and robbed shops on the popular Third Street Promenade in Santa Monica. Thieves came out of stores carrying armloads of loot and drove away unimpeded.

People came to expect this in San Francisco, where horrible city policies, like the Gascon-written Proposition 47, allowed people to shoplift anything they wanted up to $950 without being arrested and charged with a felony. According to the loony law passed by voters, nonviolent theft of items worth less than that became only a misdemeanor.

Shoplifting in San Francisco soon got so out of control that retailers began closing stores. Walgreens saw theft in San Francisco reach four times the average of its stores elsewhere in the US from 2016 to 2021. Despite spending thirty-five times more on security guards in San Francisco, the chain closed seventeen of its stores in that city. City officials blamed the problems on "organized crime." And by "organized crime" they weren't talking about the politicians whose policies encouraged it.

In Los Angeles after the Floyd riots, the city council, in the interest of "reforming the police," decided to divert $150 million from the LAPD budget for "community programs" designed to benefit the black community. The city council sought to cut the Los Angeles Unified School District police budget by $25 million. Thankfully, that lunacy didn't last. Because of the increase in crime, including shootings and homicides, the 2021 LAPD budget increased by 3 percent, and the police commission in Los Angeles asked for $213 million more for the fiscal year ending in 2023.

The pendulum started swinging back but slowly.

Policies of Democrat-run cities and states produce terrible consequences, including soft-on-crime district attorneys, the defund-the- police movement calling the police "systemically racist," and the police patrol and arrest pullback, which all cause an increase in crime. White cops reason, "Why in the world would I be proactive? There's a good chance some idiot with a smartphone films me while I'm trying to stop a crime and accuses me of 'racial profiling' or excessive use of force." And so, the police make fewer arrests, which result in more shootings and homicides, more robberies, more muggings, and more smash and grabs. People are beginning to see this simple correlation between less policing and more crime.

California will sooner or later hit rock bottom. What is rock bottom? This occurs when a homeless guy relieves himself on your front lawn—especially if that front lawn is in Bel Air, or Brentwood, or Malibu. When homelessness and crime hit the elites where they live, then we'll get change.

More and more, this is exactly what is happening.

Criminals, many of whom would be behind bars but for soft-on-crime policies, are now following rich shoppers home from the Beverly Hills stores. Crooks can get away with it because the police aren't proactive and policies like cashless bail allow bad guys to remain on the streets. Criminals know that even if they get caught, there's a good chance they won't even go to jail and if so, not for long.

In January of 2022, a rash of random killings shocked the city. A man walked up to a nurse standing at a bus stop and punched her in the head, knocking her to the ground. Hours later she died. Around the same time, a popular young female UCLA grad student, working alone at a tony Hancock Park furniture store, was stabbed to death. Homeless men with long criminal records committed both crimes. Meanwhile, in New York, a mentally ill homeless man killed a woman standing on a subway platform by pushing her onto the tracks in front of an incoming train. As the police escorted the handcuffed man away, he yelled, "I am God!"

Homelessness hurts the homeless more than anyone. If a woman is homeless on the street in Los Angeles, there's almost a 100 percent chance she will be raped--and more than once. Out there it's called "romancing."

As reported in the *Los Angeles Times,* in the summer of 2021, city personnel working over six weeks removed tents and other handmade shelters from the boardwalk and the beach, with outreach workers persuading "more than 200 people to accept shelter with the hope of eventually finding permanent housing."[10] But rather than accept the shelter that was offered, dozens of people just moved elsewhere and set up new homeless encampments. Most of the fires in Los Angeles are

10 "Block by Block, Tent by Tent, City Crews Remove Homeless Campers from Venice Beach," *Los Angeles Times,* July 8, 2021, https://www.latimes.com/homeless-housing/story/2021-07-08/it-took-two-hours-in-the-pre-dawn-darkness-for-city-crews-to-remove-one-venice-homeless-man..

started by or in homeless encampments, where there is open drug use and trafficking.

But surely drug abuse means people go to jail, right? Not in California. Gascon's Proposition 47 made possession of up to three grams of meth a misdemeanor, not a felony.

Those attempting to solve the problem say most have mental or substance abuse issues; some choose to live on the street; and some are on the street due to a lack of ability to afford housing and/or loss of a job. A 2019 Supreme Court decision, *Martin v. Boise*, left in place earlier rulings by the 9th Circuit that homeless persons cannot be punished for sleeping outside on public property in the absence of adequate alternatives. Therefore, a city has to provide an adequate alternative or street people stay where they choose on public grounds. Los Angeles failed to do that for all of the homeless. And Supreme Court case aside, many Angelenos opposed forcibly removing the homeless even if and when housing is available. Quite a problem.

One estimate puts the number of the homeless population in Los Angeles County at over sixty thousand, and notes that nearly half of the nation's homeless live in California. No one in charge of the state's cities seems to know how to effectively handle the problem, with miles and miles of people living in tents and makeshift shelters serving as a daily, growing reminder.

Not too surprisingly, working people who pay too much for housing find this disturbing, dangerous and a blot on their own neighborhoods. Try managing finally to buy a home for your family, only to watch the neighborhood become clogged with people possibly mentally ill and/or using drugs and alcohol? Business owners face homeless people camped out near their shops or sleeping in their doorways, a sight that chases away customers and profits.

The city pays Los Angeles Homelessness Services Authority (LAHSA) approximately $300 million a year. That seems like a lot, but LAHSA also gets almost $1 billion in annual funding from other sources. The agency's payroll costs in 2020 were $36.8 million. That should leave plenty of money for LAHSA to deal with the homeless in the city. Any normal person would think so.

Do the math. After payroll costs, let's say the agency has around $1.2 billion to help these homeless people, or an average of around $15,000 per person (assuming 80,000 homeless). The LAHSA.org chart, available on the agency site, lists just over 420 employee positions, 30 of them being document specialists. The agency employee's average salary is almost $88,000. This means those employees are doing more than $70,000 per person better than the homeless people they are paid to help.

That might seem understandable, except Soledad Ursua writing "L.A.'s Billion Dollar Failure" in *City Journal* in January 2022 points out that from 2015 to 2020 the number of homeless in Los Angeles grew steadily from 41,174 to 63,706, an increase of 55 percent.[11] Ursua, as a Venice Neighborhood Council board member, represents an area with a huge homeless population. She supported my campaign, as did her

---

11 Soledad Ursua, "L.A's Billion-Dollar Failure," *City Journal*, January 12, 2022, https://www.city-journal.org/los-angeles-homeless-policy-is-a-billion-dollar-failure.

mother, Gloria Molina, a Democrat and former California State Senate majority leader.

Los Angeles County sheriff Alex Villanueva essentially asked at a press conference, with $6.5 billion spent on the homeless problem over ten years, where did the money go? What did we get for it? This explains why two Democratic, Los Angeles city councilmembers, Joe Buscaino and Paul Koretz, introduced a motion for the city to withdraw from funding LAHSA. The homeless population simply isn't decreasing. For every one hundred homeless persons who moved into adequate housing, twenty replaced them on the street. The word has been out for a long time that the homeless will not be forcibly removed from public property, Supreme Court case or no, and it's easier to survive on the streets of sunny Southern California, with its generous politicians, than the cold Midwest or East Coast.

In March 2020, the city and county of Los Angeles collaborated with the state on "Project Room Key," a housing and homelessness response to the COVID-19 pandemic. It sought to minimize strain on healthcare system capacity, while providing noncongregate shelter options for people experiencing homelessness.

It failed.

"Insanity," said Sheriff Villanueva, about the policies of the Los Angeles County Board of Supervisors, the mayor of Los Angeles, and the Los Angeles city council.[12] These entities wanted deputy sheriffs to stop patrolling homeless areas,

12 Megan Gallen, "Sheriff Slams Failed Liberal Policies for LA Homeless Crisis: Year after Year of 'Insanity,'" FOX NEWS, June 10, 2021, https://www.foxnews.com/media/los-angeles-homeless-crisis-sheriff-liberal-insanity.

despite homicides increasing 186 percent since 2020. Sheriff Villanueva called the 501(c)3 nonprofit organizations that receive money from the county and the city, the ACLU attorneys who represent special interests, and the social workers who fail to solve the problem a "homeless industrial complex." In a June 23, 2021, press conference, Villanueva called LA mayor Eric Garcetti (in public office since 2001), the Los Angeles Board of Supervisors, the Los Angeles city council (representing 15 districts,) the Metro Transit Authority, and LAHSA the "architects" of Los Angeles's increasing homeless problems.

Other major cities, in and outside California—all run by Democrats—face the same problem. Homeless problems may not be the main reason people move from these cities, but they are absolutely a factor. Drive up a ramp from downtown Los Angeles, get onto the freeway going south. Watch the mile-long homeless encampments. During the campaign I was interviewed at a Hollywood hotel. The manager, a man from Kenya, introduced himself, said he intended to vote for me, pointed at a window facing the street, and said, "I moved to Los Angeles to get away from the Third World. Just one block from here it looks worse than some of the worst areas of Nairobi. Now what do I do?"

When Newsom ran for mayor of San Francisco in 2004, he said he was going to solve the homeless problem in the city in ten years. It's now much worse. When Newsom served eight years as lieutenant governor, he complained he had nothing to do. As I told audiences at my rallies, "How about fulfilling your campaign promise to the people of San Francisco and deal with the homeless?"

Dr. Ben Carson, the former secretary of the department of Housing and Urban Development (HUD), whom I consulted during my campaign, told me the problem could be solved. "We have the money to treat people," he said. "We have large areas of federal land in California. The federal government is the largest owner of land in virtually every state and certainly the largest owner of land in California. And we have already worked out a deal with the Democrat mayor of Los Angeles to use these large parcels of land to build small, low-cost housing at a fraction of the normal costs."

Livingcost.org is a crowdsourced database with a cost-of-living calculator for price comparison in 9,294 cities and 197 countries all over the world. According to their latest data as of October 2022, the one-person cost of living in California, including rent, is $2,417, which is 1.25 times more expensive than the average in the United States. California ranks as the fifth most expensive and the eleventh best state to live in the United States. The average monthly salary after taxes in California is $4,388, enough to cover one-person living expenses for 1.8 months. In Los Angeles, that cost of living is $2,865, and in San Francisco it is $3,415.

In Dallas, the cost is $2,268. In Jacksonville, Florida, you would only need $1,860 a month, making the cost of living in Los Angeles 1.54 times higher. And, again, Texas and Florida have no state income tax. In California, if you are single or married filing separately and making $48,436 to $61,214, the tax rate is 8 percent. In other words, you pay $1,672.87 plus 8 percent of the amount over $48,435.

Where do all those state income taxes go? Paying off public pensions is the fastest-growing item in the state budget.

According to CalMatters.org: "California's public employee pension dilemma boils down to this: The California Public Employees Retirement System has scarcely two-thirds of the money it needs to pay benefits that state and local governments have promised their workers. Moreover, CalPERS' official estimate is 70.8 percent funded based on an assumption of future investment earnings averaging 7 percent a year, which probably is at least one or two percentage points too high."[13]

CalPERS is the California Public Employees' Retirement System, an agency in the California executive branch that "manages pension and health benefits for more than 1.6 million California public employees, retirees, and their families." What happens to those 1.6 million employees' pensions when enough people and businesses move out of the state and the coffers get even leaner? During the campaign, I asked the media to pose that question to Newsom. They didn't.

This again brings us to job-killing regulations.

Rather than rattle off a long list of regulations and conditions that make doing business in California unfavorable to businesses, let's focus on one of the most egregious dumb actions of the state: AB 5. It went into effect January 1, 2020. The federal government notes that 55 million Americans do work as independent contractors. These are the people affected by AB 5. The law was concocted to decrease independent workers and produce more union members. Consider this AB 5 description in February 2020 from the Legislative

13 Dan Walters, "California's Immense Pension Dilemma," *Los Angeles Daily News*, August 10, 2020, https://www.dailynews.com/2020/08/10/californias-immense-pension-dilemma.

Analyst's Office, the California Legislature's Nonpartisan Fiscal and Policy Advisor:

> "New State Law Limits Who Companies Can Hire as Independent Contractors. The state recently enacted AB 5, which limits what types of work businesses can hire independent contractors to do. Specifically, the new law adopts the 'ABC' test from a recent court ruling, which requires an employer to show that its contractors: (A) work independently, (B) do work that is different from what the business does, and (C) also work for other businesses or the public. If an employer cannot show that a contractor's work meets all three parts of the test, the employer must reclassify the contractor as an employee. Due to the new test, which more strictly limits independent contractor work, many people who previously worked as independent contractors will be reclassified as employees."[14]

Here's an example. A magazine has a regular contributor, let's say a weekly columnist, who writes about pet care. The magazine, based in California, finds it economically prudent to hire the columnist as an independent contractor. The columnist gets to work from home, does not have to come into the office, deal with politics in the office, and fight traffic getting to and from there. However, under AB 5 the magazine

14 Budget and Policy Post, "Staffing to Address New Independent Contractor Test," Legislative Analyst's Office, February 11, 2020, https://lao.ca.gov/Publications/Report/4151.

must hire the columnist as a full-time employee, entitled to benefits that make the former independent contractor too expensive to hire. Lose-lose.

By the way, the ABC Test was written back in the 1930s for factory workers. But things have changed. Work conditions improved. The need for unions waned. Former AFL-CIO organizer and California assemblywoman Lorena Gonzalez, who spearheaded the disastrous bill, wore a Teamsters logo mask on the floor of the Assembly. When confronted by unhappy AB 5 victims, what was her response? "F--- Donald Trump!" she yelled at them. Gonzalez later resigned from the legislature to take a job with the California Labor Federation, a powerful group representing about 2.1 million union members.

This is, unfortunately, the kind of elected politician that is currently killing California.

BizPac Review's Vivek Saxena wrote that AB 5 "…has left thousands of state residents, including numerous single mothers and individuals with disabilities, without a source of income.… While it was originally designed to target Uber and Lyft, both of which rely heavily on freelancers for their work model, it's affected nearly every industry, including those dominated by women."[15]

Lawyer Hans Bader wrote: "AB 5 didn't work as predicted. It led mostly to firing instead of full-time hires. California companies responded to the law not by turning contractors into employees but by getting rid of them. Companies outside

---

15 Vivek Saxena, "Joe Biden's Tweet Supporting AB5 Causes Visceral Reaction from His Would-Be Supporters," *Business & Politics*, March 8, 2020, https://www.bizpacreview.com/2020/03/08/joe-bidens-tweet-supporting-ab5-causes-visceral-reaction-from-his-would-be-supporters-895336/.

California reacted to the law by refusing to hire California residents or by firing their California contractors and hiring non-California replacements."

Joe Biden endorsed the law. Newsom signed it.

Thankfully, on September 4, 2020, the legislature listened to the complaints and passed AB 2257 revising at least some of AB 5, backing off of the ABC test for advisors, content contributors, narrators, producers, and others working with publications (provided they do not displace existing employees), and others. But much damage remained, giving companies in and outside California even more reasons to do business elsewhere.

Crime, homelessness, egregious taxes, unfunded pensions, unaffordable housing, oppressive laws and regulations—if that isn't enough of a horror portrait of a state driven into the pits by politicians—how about the thing on which so many societies rise or fall?

Now we come to education. It should surprise no one that when families leave, a big reason is the detestable state of K–12 government education.

In January 2022, the *California Globe*'s Katy Grimes wrote: "Between the 2020 and 2021 school years, tens of thousands of students left California's public schools—the latest total shows more than 160,000 students have left California schools."[16]

---

16 Katy Grimes, "Proposed Education Funding Scheme Doesn't Address California's Needed Public School Reforms," California Globe, January 19, 2022, https://californiaglobe.com/articles/proposed-education-funding-scheme-doesnt-address-californias-needed-public-school-reforms.

In October 2019, the *Los Angeles Times* acknowledged the crisis:

> "Just over half of public-school students who took the state's standardized English language arts test performed at grade level, while only 4 in 10 are proficient in math, scores that represent a slow upward trend over the past four years, according to data released Wednesday by the state Department of Education.
>
> "Proficiency rates rose about 1 percentage point each in both English and math between 2018 and 2019, with 50.9 percent of students meeting English standards and 39.7 percent of students meeting math standards on the California Assessment of Student Performance and Progress, designed to test Common Core concepts. However, scores among African American students are markedly lower, prompting calls from educators to address the achievement gap."[17]

Any guess on whether those percentages improved in 2020 when the teachers used the COVID-19 pandemic to close schools in favor of online learning? A press release from the California Department of Education on January 7, 2022, had the headline "CDE Releases Student Data for 2020–21 that

17 Sonali Kohli, "Only Half of California Students Meet English Standards and Fewer Meet Math Standards, Test Scores Show," *Los Angeles Times*, October 9, 2019, https://www.latimes.com/california/story/2019-10-09/california-school-test-scores-2019.

Show Impacts of COVID-19 on Schools."[18] It conceded: "Grade-level Smarter Balanced results in math and English language arts generally show academic progress but at a slower rate than in prior years. The scores also show a widening of achievement gaps between student groups...These analyses show that the rate of gain was lower for the 2021 cohort [generational group] and that the differentials were greater for younger students than for older ones."

Pre-pandemic, nearly 70 percent of black third-grade boys could not read at state proficiency levels—which are not very high—with math scores just slightly higher. Post-pandemic, almost half of *all* third graders in California could not read at state proficiency levels, again with math scores about the same. Thanks to Newsom's teacher-union-driven shutdown. This stands in stark contrast to Florida where kids did not lose a whole year of in-person education.

Kids in California are doing worse, compared to other states, and families are moving out. To union-supported politicians like Newsom, pleasing teachers' unions wishes is more important than educating Californians.

Just as AB 5 has influenced states across the nation, other awful California practices infect other states, whether it's the state legislature's desire for "single payer" or allowing noncitizens to vote on paid family and medical leave. What happens in California often becomes a coming attraction for other states.

---

18 California Department of Education News Release, "CDE Releases Student Data for 2020–21 that Show Impacts of COVID-19 on Schools," California Department of Education, January 7, 2022, https://www.cde.ca.gov/nr/ne/yr22/yr22rel03.asp.

On the campaign trail it became evident to me that many Californians understood very little about the reasons behind rising costs and declining quality of life. They certainly knew the what, if not the why. So, I tried in my speeches and interviews to connect the dots from bad Sacramento policies to the effect in their daily lives. In eight weeks of talking and explaining, I only scratched the surface. The battle may have been lost, but I know I helped a lot of people wake up to this fact: we're in a war against bad policies that produce bad outcomes. We must keep fighting. It is imperative that we win! And like many Californians, I'm not afraid to take that fight to the front of the line.

Californians know what's happening. They know that the percentage of black people living in San Francisco and Los Angeles was higher thirty years ago. The number one reason for the outmigration? The cost-of-living rise means working-class people, a disproportionate percentage of whom are black and brown, cannot afford to stay. Yet these voters pull the lever for the very politicians who promote policies that jacked up the price of living, increased crime, and pushed them out of their hometown cities. During my campaign, when I talked to black and brown media, I said, "Connect the dots. Who's really on your side?"

Of course, connecting the dots means recognizing that Democrats lie about who they're out to help and that Republicans, if they care at all, treat the issue with complete incompetence.

California's problems were directly created by politicians elected by naïve people lied to by Democrat politicians who said one thing but did another while delivering disastrous results. Politicians pushed extreme environmental regulations that jacked up the prices of homes to the point where, as mentioned, it costs 175 percent more for a home in California compared to the average price of a home in America.

I grew up in a two-bedroom, one-bath 1,376-square-foot house in an area of South Central Los Angeles in the 90047 zip code. Look up the area on Zillow. My parents paid something like $15,000 for the home in 1959. Today it's worth almost $700,000.

That's South Central. Check out Burbank, the home of film studios like Warner Brothers, Disney, the Cartoon Network, and Nickelodeon.

Urban blacks and Hispanics bear the brunt of rising crime and failing government schools. They're the ones who can't buy a house because of the cost of living due, in part, to misguided left-wing policies, rules, and regulations. They're the ones disproportionately suffering from inflation-driven high prices for gas and food.

As I've said before, look at the demographics of people in San Francisco thirty years ago. The percentage of blacks was much higher than in 2022. It's the same in Los Angeles, and families can't afford the Golden State life they dreamed of because of the policies they supported by voting for Democrats.

We can change this. I got off the sidelines after being a talk show host for twenty seven years because I couldn't stand to see the cost of government dysfunction in my state. Now, I see others running for office around the country, many saying my campaign inspired them to do so. Yes, your personal life gets scrutinized. People flat out lie in order to get others to hate you. But it's worth it, when the state—and the country—is quite literally at stake.

Chapter 5

WHAT I LEARNED FROM MY CAMPAIGN

CALIFORNIA IS A LIBERAL STATE, and Gavin Newsom had been elected in 2018 by a wide margin, beating Republican John Cox with 62 percent of the vote. So why did so many Californians feel the need to remove this apparently popular governor from office just a couple years later?

For some, it was Newsom's rank hypocrisy. It was bad enough that businesses across the state were forced to shut down due to COVID-19 mandates. But then he was caught dining maskless at the very expensive French Laundry restaurant in northern California, while also incurring a $12,000 wine tab picked up by the taxpayers. I don't know what he was drinking but I can assure you it wasn't Mad Dog 20/20.

A recent study by the Cato Institute, the libertarian think tank, ranked California forty-eighth out of the fifty states in personal and economic freedom. The study also examined fiscal and regulatory policy. For the first time, California's population decreased in 2021, resulting in the loss of a congressional seat. In the third quarter, more people on average left the state versus sixty thousand net departures in the first quarter of 2020.

Between March 2020 and September 2021, there had been a 38 percent decrease in new arrivals. California has fifty-eight counties, and new arrivals fell in every single one.

Meanwhile the California Department of Education had proposed an "equitable math" framework. According to *California Political Review*, the framework "promotes the concept that working to figure out a correct answer is an example of racism and white supremacy invading the classroom."

But even as Democratic lawmakers sought to protect our children from harmful and outdated stereotypes, many kids educated in California public schools could not read or perform math at state levels of proficiency—standards that were not particularly high. In 2019 barely half of kids in public schools were reading-proficient, while only 40 percent were math-proficient.

In December 2021, California's jobless rate of 7.3 percent tied with Nevada's for worst in the nation. Texas and Florida clocked in at 5.4 percent and 4.6 percent. UCLA economist Lee Ohanian co-authored an August 2021 report on the tax and regulatory policies causing businesses to ditch California at an unprecedented rate. The report found that "unless policy reforms reverse this course, California will continue to lose businesses, both large established businesses, as well as young, rapidly growing businesses, some of which will become transformational giants of tomorrow."

In a population of almost 40 million Californians, 1 percent of taxpayers accounted for nearly half of the state's income tax revenues.

California policies are expelling rich high-profilers. Elon Musk, currently one of the two richest men in the world, announced he was relocating his Tesla headquarters from California to Texas. Musk, who said that he would pay $11 billion in taxes that year—depriving the state of over $1 billion in state income tax in just one year—had already moved his residence from Los Angeles to Austin. His departure was followed by that of popular podcaster Dave Rubin and the brilliant conservative commentator and *Daily Wire* co-founder, Ben Shapiro, who relocated his operations to Tennessee and his residence to Florida.

Good people from all walks of life in California agreed—something had to be done. Someone who could motivate and inspire people had to step forward. The idea for a recall was the result of a groundswell of discontent with Newsom. While every California governor since 1960 has faced some form of recall attempt—and one actually succeeded in 2003—the attempt on Newsom was pushed to the brink by the French Laundry incident. When the recall petition was certified in July, the state was in a frenzy. Forty-five candidates threw their hats into the ring, including the former Olympian Caitlyn Jenner, former representative Doug Ose, the businessman John Cox, then assemblyman Kevin Kiley, and Kevin Faulconer, who had just wrapped up his tenure as mayor of San Diego. This huge cast of characters drove a feeding frenzy for the state and national press, which almost uniformly rallied to the defense of the governor.

As I watched the momentum for the recall build, it was not my first impulse to run. All things considered, I was doing pretty well as a talk radio host and media producer. So why did I decide to run for governor? Running for office had never been my ambition. But four main people inspired me to try.

The first was Ginny Sand, the wife of Larry Sand, president of the nonprofit California Teachers Empowerment Network. All I knew about Ginny was that she was a local activist who kept writing to me and urging me to run. How she got my personal email, I never knew. But she wrote long letters about why I should run, how I could do it, and how much money I could raise.

I told my girlfriend, Nina, "Let's just sit down for a few minutes for coffee with Ginny and get her off my back." So we agreed to have a twenty-minute coffee klatch. After a four-hour sit-down at a nearby restaurant, Ginny supplied me with stacks of written material on the issues facing California and a strategy for winning. In a state where registered Republicans are outnumbered by registered Democrats two-to-one, she said she had calculated scenarios where I could get just enough of the vote to knock down Newsom. She had talked to two hundred thirty activists leaders up and down the state, all of whom said I had a good shot. The meeting got me thinking... and thinking...and praying.

Next was my longtime friend and fellow Salem Radio Network talk show host Dennis Prager. If it weren't for Dennis, I wouldn't be on the radio today, so I rate his opinion very highly. He gave me a well-reasoned pitch about why, even as an outsider and political novice, I should challenge Newsom in the 2021 election. Dennis believes that there are four qualities that make a great man: courage, truthfulness, a willingness not to be loved, and to be an outlier. He told me I possessed all four. "All great people are outliers," Dennis said. "Not every outlier does good, but all good is achieved by outliers—people who march to their own, or God's, drum."

My interest grew further when my pastor, Jack Hibbs of Calvary Chapel Chino Hills in southern California, sent me a video from Boston. I met Jack several years previously when we were looking for a new church. He is a force of nature. The product of a botched abortion, he became a pastor after a successful career as a businessman. Talking to him reminded me of that line in the book of Esther, "for a time such as this"—and eventually that sentiment became something of a campaign theme. Throughout my whole life, faith has been important, but especially so at that moment.

Shortly before I announced, Jack and three busloads of parishioners were in Boston visiting Bunker Hill, the starting place of the American Revolution. Jack and his wife, Lisa, had grown their church from a home fellowship of six worshippers into one that ministers weekly to over ten thousand people and millions worldwide through daily media programs. Married for over forty years, Jack and Lisa co-wrote a book, *Turn Around at Home: Giving a Stronger Spiritual Legacy Than You Received.*

It was their last day in Boston, and on the brief video, with cheering parishioners standing behind him, Pastor Jack told me in no uncertain terms "to fight for what's right." He added: "And make sure that we have a governor that represents the people of California. Larry, we need you to run for governor. We've got a nation to save. And I want to remind you that there's a whole lot of people. We've got senators that are behind you, congressmen that are behind you. If anyone has a foot up on this run, it's you. And we want to remind you that you are so electable. Larry, you have come from the trenches of South Central Los Angeles. You have, by God's grace, a successful awesome blessed life. Your narrative, your story, your life is perfect for such a time as this."

Then Jack led his parishioners in prayer for me. "Father, in Jesus's name. Honestly, Lord, we don't know when to persuade him because we want your calling to be upon him from the Throne Room of Heaven because this is not a coincidence that these momentary Bostonians soon to be back-to-Californians are praying for Larry Elder and for his success, and, maybe God, You might touch his heart to say, if I don't do this, I will be in disobedience. Lord, would you touch Larry to throw off comfort and to realize that this is the moment of life and death, for our state is in the death throes, a grip of anarchy and tyranny. Father, maybe there's hope while we're still alive. We ask you, God, to bless our brother Larry, and, Father, continue to go before him and by all means remember what you started in the 1700s and do it again. In Jesus's name, Amen!"

Goodness, I thought to myself. Boston. I thought of the Boston Tea Party, Paul Revere, and especially Crispus Attucks, the black sailor who stood in the front line of a group of fifty patriots defying British troops. Attucks was the first American killed in the Revolution, by two bullets in his chest, at what became known as the Boston Massacre. He was the first of five thousand black soldiers who fought for an independent America. Maybe Pastor Jack wasn't thinking of Attucks when he sent that video, but I thought of him, and the implications had an impact.

The fourth influential person who urged me to run was my friend Lionel Chetwynd, a successful and talented writer and filmmaker whom I'd known for thirty years.

Lionel called and asked to come to my house. He said he had "urgent business" to discuss. The urgent business was his request that I run for governor. Lionel, a conservative producer, director, and writer, had received an Academy Award–nomination for best adapted screenplay for *The Apprenticeship of Duddy Kravitz.* He directed the critically acclaimed *The Hanoi Hilton.* Given Lionel's sixty long form and feature credits and over two dozen documentary credits, nominated and awarded, his opinion mattered. He sat down and told me that I had a moral and ethical obligation to do this and that I would be thumbing my nose at God if I didn't. So, by the time he left my house, I was pretty much sold.

But I still said, wait. Let me ask some normal people. So I floated the idea with my barber, the guy who had cut my hair for thirty years.

"Kelly," I said, "People want me to run for governor."

I thought, or perhaps hoped, he would say, "Larry, you have a great life. You make good money. What do you need this bullshit for?"

Much to my surprise, Kelly said, "You should do it, Larry. Do it!"

My friend Ed owns a limo service, and for years I've used his drivers. Every now and then he personally drives me. Let me ask him. Again, I thought for sure he'd say, "Larry, you have a great life, what do you need this for?" But no.

"You should do it!" he shouted as he looked at me in the rearview mirror. "Run and save us!"

Save us?

"You can turn this state around, Larry. You can do it. You've got common sense. You've got good judgment. Turn this place around!"

So, there it was. Close long-time friends, my pastor, and now hard-working normal people telling me to go for it. Far from any impulse to achieve fame or power, I began to feel a moral, spiritual, and patriotic duty to run. I also felt that if I didn't, I would regret it for the rest of my life. I feared sitting on the sidelines, watching the recall fail and saying to myself, "Larry, just maybe, you could have won this thing."

Actually running, however, proved much more difficult than it should have been.

I announced my candidacy on July 12, in Norwalk, a suburb of Los Angeles, only to be blocked by state election officials who said I had filed incomplete federal tax return information. They wanted to keep me off the ballot and I had to fight it out in court.

I raised $22 million in less than eight weeks from people all over the country. While this was far short of Newsom's huge fund, it was several times more than what my advisors thought I could raise. And it was more than all my Republican rivals combined, including John Cox, who made his money in investment counseling and had already run against Newsom in 2018, funded with millions of dollars of his own money. Now the law in California does allow the amount above $9 million to be spent by an "independent expenditure" committee—but the money cannot be used in an ad that says, "Vote

Elder." It can be used in ads arguing why Newsom should be recalled. Such ads will have a tag at the end that says something like "Larry Elder expenditure committee"—but not a direct "vote for Elder" solicitation.

I did not expect to immediately become the frontrunner when I announced my candidacy. And my lead only increased every time they had a Republican debate. I ended up carrying 57 of the 58 counties on the replacement side. The only one I didn't carry was San Francisco. I only lost by 149 votes, and we didn't spend one dime of advertising or one minute campaigning there. If I had spent time there, I would have carried that county as well. I carried San Diego, where Kevin Faulconer had been mayor, by thirty points. The Sacramento area is Kevin Kiley territory, who managed to get elected to Congress in 2022—and I carried his county by thirty points.

What did I think about my opponents that I didn't say during the race? Well, I don't know what Caitlyn Jenner was thinking. Jenner won a lot of media attention, but little outside of that. Many said she ran a vanity campaign, and she did little to combat the perception. During the campaign, she went to Australia to compete on the country's television series *Big Brother VIP*. In the end, she won less than 1 percent of the vote. After the campaign, some said, "The reason you did so well is because you have high name recognition." I replied, "Higher than Caitlyn Jenner?" As for multimillionaire Cox, he had run some five times for various offices, never winning.

A wealthy friend whom I thought would donate the maximum $32,400 to me for my gubernatorial campaign initially declined. When I approached him, he said he was going with Faulconer. I asked why. He told me the job required experience,

Faulconer having been a two-term mayor of San Diego. I told him he bet on the wrong horse. A month into the campaign. I became the number one replacement candidate—by far. I went back to the donor. He said I had been right. He wrote me a full check for the max. He even told me that he told Faulconer to knock off his "bullshit" attacks against me. "Larry is the only one that has a chance to beat Newsom," he said, "There's no need for us to be cutting each other up. Knock it off."

"When I campaign, I'm a uniter," I said.

Years ago, I discussed running for US Senate with Arnold Schwarzenegger and former Los Angeles mayor Richard Riordan, at their invitation. We met at Riordan's home. They wanted me to run against Senator Barbara Boxer, D-California I agreed to do it on one condition: the national GOP had to endorse me.

I flew to Washington, DC, where I met with, among other Republican senators, John Cornyn, the head of the committee in charge of recruiting senate candidates. But the national GOP endorsed Carly Fiorina. I never flirted with the idea of running for political office before or since—until the recall.

During the campaign I never reached out to Schwarzenegger. Nor did he reach out to me. He was very unpopular when he left office. California conservatives who supported him felt double-crossed. I am one of them. He won the 2003 recall race (the only successful gubernatorial recall campaign in state history) against Gray Davis because of an unpopular automobile tax increase. By the end of his administration, Schwarzenegger had actually raised that same car tax and become a climate change alarmist. As a Schwarzenegger-advocate on radio, I felt I let my listeners down by pushing for him during that election. I supported him over conservative Representative Tom McClintock, whom I preferred ideologically, but felt didn't have as good a chance to win as Schwarzenegger.

I got outspent nearly ten-to-one by the Newsom campaign. But this time, he spent 50 percent more per voter to keep his job than he spent to get his job. Newsom spent more money in the recall compared to his 2018 election. He spent nearly six dollars per vote in 2018. He spent nine dollars per vote in the recall.

The media, my replacement rivals, and Newsom underestimated my popularity. So did I! Who knew that from the moment I announced my candidacy, I'd become the front-runner and my lead, according to the polls, would grow each week?

Evidently the polls scared Newsom, so he turned to Hollywood, Silicon Valley, and other big players. One month before the recall election, an August 2021 *Hollywood Reporter* headline read: "Facing Recall, Gavin Newsom Calls on Hollywood Dems: Help!" Those called on included Steven Spielberg, Reed Hastings, "and other left-leaning moguls to contribute big money and to mobilize Democrats."

Newsom's aides asked drug-addled rapper Snoop Dogg to tweet against me to his nearly 20 million followers despite my support for school choice, which benefits kids and parents in the inner city where Calvin "Snoop Dog" Broadus grew up. Either he's too dumb or too high to care.

The chairman of Netflix, Reed Hastings, gave $3 million to an antirecall political action committee. According to the secretary of state's office, Democratic megadonor Steven

Spielberg only put in $25,000, while his former DreamWorks partner, Jeffrey Katzenberg, gave Newsom $500,000. Haim Saban, the man who got rich on Power Rangers, put in $50,000. Black entertainment mogul Byron Allen contributed $10,000, and Barbra Streisand gave a mere $2,500.

Silicon Valley people, whose Leftism is often indistinguishable from the Hollywood types, gave even more. Priscilla Chan of Facebook, Laurene Powell Jobs (Steve Jobs's widow), and former Google CEO Eric Schmidt all contributed six-figure amounts. Paramount Pictures gave $40,000, and NBC donated $25,000.

Why was Newsom so worried?

The Hollywood Reporter said he needed "more than celebrity tweets to get him out of this jam."[19] The paper cited a *RealClearPolitics* polling average that showed the percentage of voters who supported recalling Newsom exceeded the percentage of those who opposed it. As of August 24, 2021, the numbers were 48 percent for recall to 47.5 percent against. That's why I kept telling anyone who would listen, "We had a real shot."

Newsom raised $1 million in a Zoom call with a dozen Hollywood people including Byron Allen, Jeffrey Katzenberg, Rob and Michelle Reiner, and Alan and Cindy Horn. Alan, at the time, was the chief creative officer of Disney Studios Content.

In addition to Hollywood, Newsom called on Barack Obama, Senator Bernie Sanders, D-Vermont, and Senator Elizabeth Warren, D-Oklahoma, to cut commercials for him.

---

19 Peter Kiefer, "Facing Recall, Gavin Newsom Calls on Hollywood Dems: Help!" *The Hollywood Reporter*, August 25, 2021, https://www.hollywoodreporter.com/news/politics-news/gavin-newsom-recall-hollywood-democrats-help.

Obama said: "Now Republicans are trying to recall him from office and overturn common-sense COVID safety measures for healthcare workers and school staff...Protect California by voting 'No' on the Republican recall."[20]

Sanders said: "The absolute last thing we need at this unprecedented moment in American history is some right-wing Republican governor in California trying to impede the president's agenda."[21]

Warren said: "We've seen Trump Republicans across the country attacking election results and the right to vote. Now they're coming to grab power in California...Stop the Republican recall!"[22]

Biden flew out to California and campaigned with Newsom. Before Biden took the stage, Newsom said: "We may have defeated Donald Trump, but we have not defeated Trumpism. Trumpism is still on the ballot in California."[23] Biden said: "I got to run against the real Donald Trump. Well, this year, the leading Republican running for governor is the closest thing

20 Dan Merica, "Obama Says California Recall Vote Is Difference 'Between Protecting our Kids and Putting Them at Risk' in New TV Ad," CNN, September 8, 2021, https://www.cnn.com/2021/09/08/politics/barack-obama-california-recall-tv-ad.

21 Bernie Sanders, Twitter post, September 10, 2021, 5:33 p.m., https://twitter.com/BernieSanders/status/1436457707733753875?s=20&t=gfTDFuuBOSc77QSryzfRyg.Bernie.

22 Tal Axelrod, "Warren Hits the Airwaves for Newsom Ahead of Recall Election," *The Hill*, July 28, 2021, https://thehill.com/homenews/campaign/565285-warren-hits-the-air-waves-for-newsom-ahead-of-recall-election/.

23 Dan Merica, "Biden Links Elder to Trump on Eve of California Recall," CNN, September 14, 2021, https://www.cnn.com/2021/09/13/politics/newsom-biden-california-recall.

to a Trump clone that I've ever seen." Although he didn't say my name, Biden was referring to me.

All told, an impressive turnout. Yet revealingly, not one of the Newsom advocates said: "Gavin Newsom has done a good job for the people of California."

Obama's help was particularly ironic when one considers that Newsom's terrible policies hurt blacks the most. In the last thirty years or so, the percentage of blacks living in Los Angeles and San Francisco declined because the home price index in California climbed to $800,000 by October, 2021, 149 percent above the *national average.* While 6.5 percent of California is black, according to HUD, nearly 40 percent of California's homeless population is black. Gavin Newsom promised to end homelessness in San Francisco when he ran for mayor. It only got worse.

Did Obama not care that, prepandemic, nearly 70 percent of black third graders in California government schools couldn't read at state proficiency levels? Or that polls show black and Hispanic parents want school choice? Both Obama and his kids enjoyed K–12 private education. What about all the kids in the underperforming California government schools, where almost 80 percent of the students are black, Hispanic, Asian, or multiracial? School choice was a centerpiece of my campaign. Newsom, whose largest campaign contributors are the powerful labor unions—including teachers' unions—oppose school choice.

But, of course, the facts didn't matter. That became abundantly clear from some of the negative articles on my candidacy. The *New York Times,* for example, ran a piece that never mentioned my race, let alone that I stood to become

California's first black governor. Fine with me. Isn't it about time we pay more attention to a candidate's suitability rather than the identity box he or she checks? But on the very same day, the *New York Times* wrote about Kathy Hochul, the new governor of New York, enthusiastically noting that she became that state's "first female" governor after Governor Andrew Cuomo was forced to retire in disgrace. With a "D" next to her name, her being "the first" became relevant to the *New York Times.* But to this national "newspaper of record" the "R" after my name meant that I ceased being black.

Over one hundred and fifty thousand people donated to my campaign, the majority of whom lived outside the state. Why so many outside donors, many of whom never even lived in California? They agreed with this long-standing adage in American politics: As goes California, so goes the nation.

Throughout the campaign, I tried to stay focused on what I could do to make California better. In some stops the positive energy was palpable. At one event in Thousand Oaks, outside Los Angeles, I was mobbed by a huge crowd of people, so tight that I could hardly breathe. It was like the Beatles had come to town. Security was all around me, but I never felt unsafe. All these people were in a good mood and they were all onboard with the mission.

But other times, it took all I had to keep my sense of humor. When I was attacked on the street in Venice, California, by a white woman wearing a gorilla mask, who threw an egg at me, it drew headlines like, "White woman in gorilla mask throws egg at Larry Elder." Asked about it later, I joked, "Hey, how do you know it was a mask?" Then I would pause and say, "Maybe she was having a bad hair day."

Days earlier, at another press conference held in a restaurant, the owner of a tavern in Sherman Oaks denounced the reporter who called me "the black face of white supremacy." The owner said, "You call somebody that, it's the kind of thing that can get people killed."

And forty-five minutes before the egg attack, we got shot at. At this street press conference, a car drove by and someone inside fired two shots, hitting one of my security guards in the back, hurting him but not seriously. Another security guard was holding a folder and a bullet went through it. Turned out the shots came from a pellet gun. Someone could have been blinded. We reported this to the police but continued campaigning without publicly saying a word about the pellet attack. We feared copycats.

The next day, the *Los Angeles Times* wrote about the egg attack with the headline: "Elder Involved in Altercation in Venice." It included a photo of me embracing a campaign supporter, a member of the Venice Neighborhood Council who was accompanying me as we toured the homeless encampment. But the *Los Angeles Times* froze our embrace so it appeared as if I was slapping her.[24]

So, if you saw the headline "Elder Involved in Altercation in Venice" and didn't read the article, you could easily assume that the altercation was me slapping a young woman. It looked hideous. The supporters in the picture contacted the

24 Mary Margaret Olohan, "Larry Elder's Campaign Slams LA Times Photo 'That Made It Appear' He was "Hitting Supporter," *Daily Caller*, September 10, 2021, https://dailycaller.com/2021/09/10/larry-elders-campaign-slams-la-times-over-photo-that-made-it-appear-he-was-hitting-supporter/.

Los Angeles Times and complained like hell. The *Los Angeles Times* removed the picture but kept the headline.

No matter what I did or said, I couldn't catch a break with the media. Asked about COVID-19, I said that people who are in high-risk categories because of their age or underlying comorbidities absolutely ought to be vaccinated. Young, healthy people not likely to get sick or to be hospitalized, not likely to die, shouldn't be forced. CNN sent reporter Joe Johns to interview me about it. We interviewed for about a half hour. They played the part where I said that young, healthy people need not be vaccinated, and that children aren't likely to get sick, get hospitalized and are certainly not likely to die. Johns, in a voice-over response said, "But that's not true, according to the CDC." Really? In the long run, who turned out to be right?

Soon the line was that Larry Elder is "antivax."

I didn't get much fairness from my Republican opponents either. I was repeatedly invited to debate my Republican rivals. I refused. There was a lot of pressure for me to participate in the first debate, including from Hugh Hewitt, a co-debate moderator and a fellow Salem Network syndicated radio host. Hewitt insisted that I had an obligation to attend the debate, and it ticked me off that he wouldn't let it go when I told him that I was not going to do it. I had two objections. Number one, I was doing fundraisers almost every night. On the night of that debate, I raised $300,000. In one night.

Number two, "What's the point of debating fellow Republicans?" I asked Hewitt. "We Republicans all know the major issues and I choose not to engage in a circular firing squad. All we're going to do is produce video and audio for Newsom to use against us in attack ads."

It didn't make any sense.

Hewitt insisted that not enough people knew me. He said if I "did the debate and performed well—and you will—people who don't know you will suddenly know you."

I asked if he sincerely believed that people who were Democrats or independents were going to watch that debate. "The only people that are gonna watch the debate are people like you," I told him. "And they already know who I am. I'm not doing it."

Hewitt even said he'd leave a chair, empty or not, for me at the debate. It pissed me off. I called Salem management and they were very supportive of me. They gave the maximum allowable contribution to my campaign as well.

"Why is he doing this? It's about him," I told Salem, "because he's comoderating the debate."

Hewitt backed off.

So, the debate was held without me. Even so, my poll numbers increased after that debate and grew after every Republican debate—there were about four—despite my absence. Meanwhile, the only person I wanted to debate was Newsom. And while he was invited, he, of course, refused to participate.

At one of the Republican debates, a moderator dredged up a column I wrote over twenty years ago and used it out-of-context to make the charge that, "Larry Elder said women are dumber than men."

But Republican candidate Kevin Faulconer pounced. "That's bullshit!" he snapped and proceeded to denounce me.[25] Later, he held a press conference with four or five women that he had apparently paid to appear. At that conference Faulconer boasted about being prowoman, while implying that I was somehow antiwoman.

(The article in question was over twenty years old and called "The SHE Issues"—with "SHE" standing for Social Security, Healthcare, and Education.[26] In it, I quoted a left-wing female professor from the left-wing University of Pennsylvania Annenberg School of Communication who said the reason that women know less than men about political issues is that they get most of their news from watching local news and—her quote—"Watching local news makes you dumber." I didn't say it. I just quoted her in my article.)

I've also written that young women are more likely to be in college than young men, and young women make more money than young men—but that didn't fit the moderator's script.

Frankly, this incident illustrated one of the many reasons I was hesitant to run, because I knew there was a whole lot of my material out there. I'd been on radio for twenty-seven years. That's about twenty-seven thousand hours, twelve hundred columns, and countless TV and radio interviews. With

25 Dustin Gardiner, "Newsom Recall: Faulconer Calls Larry Elder's Comments About Women 'Indefensible,'" *San Francisco Chronicle*, August 17, 2021, https://www.sfchronicle.com/politics/article/Newsom-recall-Faulconer-denounces-Larry.

26 Larry Elder, "Democrats and the 'SHE' Vote," *Capitalism* Magazine, May 5, 2000, https://www.capitalismmagazine.com/2000/05/democrats-and-the-she-vote/.

that much material, it's not hard to find something that can be whittled down to a sixty-second ad and taken out of context to make me look like a madman. Frankly, I was surprised at how little ammunition they could find. A twenty-year-old article where I quoted a left-wing study? Really?

Thankfully, Faulconer's attack didn't hurt me. To the contrary, it made me look good. For example, during the recall, California GOP Representative Darryl Issa and I appeared on CNN, where the host played something that I said on radio about women who were protesting sexual harassment. Referring to three or four not particularly attractive, middle-aged women holding up signs denouncing sexual harassment, I said, "Well, you guys don't have a whole lot to worry about."

"Larry's been on the air for all these years," Issa pointed out. "This is all you got? Larry was just being funny. He was just being sarcastic. I mean, this is what he does for a living."

Issa added, "When Elder entered the race, he automatically doubled the IQ of everybody else."

Then in September, there was a bombshell. Newsom and some of my Republican rivals attacked me with an accusation of being "antiwomen." This was supposedly based on two things. A former fiancée alleged that I "waved a gun at her."[27] The only thing she said that was true is that she was an ex. I've never waved a gun, loaded or unloaded, at anyone.

She also claimed she broke off the engagement. No, I did. She also claimed she was so afraid of me while I engaged

---

27 Carla Marinucci, "Elder's Ex-Fiancée Said He Brandished a Gun at Her," *POLITICO,* August 19, 2021, https://www.politico.com/news/2021/08/19/elders-ex-fiancee-said-he-brandished-a-gun-at-her-506286.

in a verbal tirade over her ending our relationship that she locked herself in my bathroom. In fact, I locked myself in my own bathroom at least twice when she attacked me verbally because I had broken off the engagement.

She called me everything but a child of God in hopes, in my opinion, of goading me to do something as stupid as physically attack her. That was about seven years ago. And, after hiring an eviction lawyer to get her out of my house, I never spoke to or communicated with her in any way, not even by carrier pigeon, ever again.

Before my campaign, I sat down with Jeff Corless, my campaign manager, and my pastor and told them all the things I could think of that I've ever done that might cause a problem when the media or my political enemies tried to find something, anything, to attack me with. I told them about my ex-girlfriend and said there was no telling what she might say or do. As to the gun-waving allegation, most media outlets initially refused to publish it. After all, it was a "she said, he said" thing. And she never went to the police for my alleged criminal act because it never happened. But *Politico*, arguably the only outlet more hostile to me than the *Los Angeles Times*, published her baseless allegation nonetheless. Then the other left-wing outlets began reporting on *Politico*'s reporting. That's how the media rolls. As with the fake Steele dossier, the media waits until an irresponsible media outlet like *Buzzfeed* "reports" something; then the rest feel free to report on their reporting.

After I was finally able to rid my life of the woman, she managed to move into an apartment owned and run by the St. Sofia Greek Orthodox Church on the eastside of Los Angeles.

When the head of the church, whom I've known for nearly fifteen years, heard about the allegation, he put out an unsolicited statement. I never asked him to say anything because I did not want to draw him into the controversy. But he contacted me, told me that she was "unstable" and that he would publicly say so. He put out a statement accusing her of being unstable; that while she complained to him about me, she never told him of any gun-waving incident; that she lied to him about her supposed intention to join his church; and that as a tenant she made bogus complaints about her apartment in order to get out of paying rent.

When the "news" about her accusations broke, I told my campaign that I would take a polygraph disputing all her allegations. My campaign manager talked me out of it. "If you do that, you'll have to take a polygraph over assertions by anyone and everyone for the rest of your political career," he said. I offered to take it just for my campaign staffers, not for public consumption. "I would not want to work for someone," I told them, "If I had any inkling that any of that stuff was true." They insisted that they knew me well enough to know the truth.

At a rally at the Pacific Club in Newport Beach, yet another emergency erupted. Several female donors rushed over to Nina. "Why are you registered as a Democrat?" one said. "What in the world are you talking about?" Nina replied. "Arnold Schwarzenegger's wife, Maria Shriver, was a registered Democrat," she said. "And when Schwarzenegger became governor after the recall, she pulled him so far to the Left we might as well have let the Democrat stay in office. We're not going through that again—letting a wife or, in Larry's case, his girlfriend—push him to the Left."

"I assure you," Nina said. "I am a conservative registered Republican, always have been. There must be a 'Nina Perry' who is a Democrat. That's not me. I used to be an actress and started using the name Nina Perry. But my real name is Terry Lynn Pohorski. Check for a voter registered in Los Angeles County under that name." The women laughed, and one said, "Goodness! That's a relief." An hour later one told Nina, "We checked. You're right. It's under Terry Lynn Pohorski." She leaned over to Nina and whispered, "I don't blame you for changing it."

Now to the bombshell.

Former actress and #MeToo activist Rose McGowan officially endorsed me in an interview with Dave Rubin, a friend and conservative gay YouTuber with a big following. McGowan said that Gavin Newsom's ex-wife, Jennifer Siebel Newsom, called Rose—before the Harvey Weinstein scandal broke—on behalf of Weinstein's attorney David Boies to try to bribe her into staying silent about her allegation that Weinstein raped her. It was Rose's allegation that triggered other women into coming forward to make similar allegations against Weinstein.

Rubin informed her that Siebel is not Newsom's ex-wife, but that the two remain married. Rose contacted my campaign and offered to hold a press conference with me in which she would accuse Newsom's wife, supposedly all about women's rights, of attempting to protect an alleged rapist. Newsom's wife, Rose claimed, contacted her and said something to the effect of "what can we do to make this go away." Rose even had emails from Seibel to corroborate the claim that she wanted to negotiate a deal in exchange for Rose's silence.

If Elder is antiwoman, what do you call this? And are we supposed to believe that Newsom himself was unaware of his wife's outreach to McGowan? If not, what is the "prowoman" governor's opinion? Surely the media would ask questions. But, for the most part, there was media silence. Yes, media outlets attended our joint press conference. But the headlines mirrored the one in the *Los Angeles Times*: "Rose McGowan Stumps for Elder, Slams Newsom at Recall Event." Stumps for Elder? In *Politico,* Carla Marinucci wrote "Accusations Fly" as opposed to "Gavin Newsom's wife tried to pay off Rose McGowan to get her to back off the Harvey Weinstein rape story." The media didn't give a damn.

If the media responded to scurrilous events in the interest of investigating them, that would be one thing, but a conservative can't expect fair treatment. I have zero confidence that the media will care enough to look into such things about liberals they want to protect.

At least we got a fair shake in *Newsweek* where Emma Nolan wrote, "Rose McGowan Posts Alleged Email from Gavin Newsom's Wife After Governor Disputes Claims."[28] Four tweets written by Rose elaborating on her claim about Mrs. Newsom were included in the article.

Nolan described Rose as "the former 'Charmed' star, who was a leading figure in the #MeToo movement." Claiming

---

28 Emma Nolan, "Rose McGowan Posts Alleged Email from Gavin Newsom's Wife After Governor Disputes Claims," *Newsweek*, September 13, 2021, https://www.newsweek.com/rose-mcgowan-posts-alleged-email-gavin-newsom-wife-governor-disputes-claims-weinstein-1628364.

Rose's expose was a "complete fabrication," Mrs. Newsom's spokesperson said: "It's disappointing but not surprising to see political opponents launch these false attacks just days before the election. Their [meaning Jennifer and Rose's] limited correspondence has been strictly as fellow survivors of sexual assault and in Jennifer's former capacity leading the Representation Project, an organization that fights limiting gender stereotypes and norms."

Newsweek reached out to the governor and Newsom dismissed the claims as a "last-minute classic hit piece." The article said that in speaking to the Associated Press, Newsom said the allegations against his wife "just shows you how low things go in campaigns these days."

But at the time, all the momentum seemed to be in my favor. Mike Piazza, Los Angeles Dodger baseball great and Hall of Famer, endorsed me in a video. He said if I got elected, he would appear at Dodger Stadium to thank everyone. "When I first got to LA," he said in his video, "all my friends talked about moving to California. And now, all everyone talks about is moving out of California. Larry Elder wants to change this. He's a man who deeply loves California and will bring back the California dream."[29]

Even though it became patently obvious early on that I was leaving the pack of other Republican candidates far behind, elected California Republican politicians—with a few exceptions—did not endorse me. The state GOP did not. Only

29 David Aaro, "Mike Piazza's Video Pitch for Larry Elder Fails to Sway California Voters to Oust Newsom in Recall Election," FOX NEWS, September 15, 2021, https://www.foxnews.com/sports/mike-piazza-video-larry-elder-california-voters-newsom-recall-election.

two members of the House congressional delegation, Doug LaMalfa and Michelle Steele, officially endorsed me. Darrell Issa had positive things to say about me, and let me take a picture with him, but he officially endorsed Kevin Faulconer. California politicians stayed out of the recall at the behest of Republican House minority leader Kevin McCarthy, who felt the recall was a loser and that Republicans should husband their money and energy.

Many local Republican Party members felt otherwise. In August, Fred Whitaker, chairman of the Orange County GOP, endorsed me. The *Orange County Register* also endorsed me.

Actor Jon Voight supported me, attended some of my rallies, but initially did not make an official announcement, although he did allow me to take pictures with him and post them on social media. When Clint Eastwood contacted me with a message of his support, I tweeted: "A shout out to Mr. Eastwood. You made my day." Chuck Norris gave me his endorsement as did Dean "Superman" Cain who tweeted: "My idea is to speak loudly about those principles and values and give my support to candidates like Larry Elder."[30]

In September, Jon Voight, in a video, officially endorsed me: "My fellow Americans, we are in a disgusting war of left-wing mentality. How can we live with our children being exposed to this Left, our governor Newsom, and his demands for shots? How can we be taken down by such wrongdoing against our freedom, our rights as humans, as Americans? Let us vote for Elder, Larry Elder. Let our states be saved with

30 Dean Cain, Twitter post, August 2, 2022, 12:29 p.m., https://twitter.com/RealDeanCain/status/1422248301622042625?s=20&t=Ju6azF6EfnQ41FBMa8VZ8A.

truths, with a force of God's rules, not leftist rules that will destroy our young. I will stand for Elder. I will ask all to vote for this man of dignity, of truths, not of power, not of lies."[31]

That was humbling to hear.

The real political shocker, however, came from the "other side of the aisle" when Gloria Romero, a Latina and former Democratic majority leader for the California State Senate, said: "Yes, I'm a Democrat. But the recall of Newsom is not about political parties. It's about Newsom. Larry Elder for governor."[32] In a video my campaign released, Romero said: "Our public schools need big change. I'm Gloria Romero; I was the majority leader of Democrats in the state Senate. I believe in charter schools and school choice. So does Larry Elder—but not Gavin Newsom. He shut our public schools while he sent his kids to private schools."

Where Newsom and the Democrats had the big edge, even bigger than the pro-Democrat/anti-Republican media, was, of course, with money. Lots of it. Going into the race, I had no idea how much money I could raise. When I wasn't giving a print, radio or television interview or attending a rally, I was on the phone asking for money. I had restrictions. But Newsom—who was not a candidate—did not. He could spend an unlimited amount of money—and did.

31 Anders Anglesey, "Jon Voight Champions Larry Elder to Replace Newsom: 'Let Us Rid This Horror,'" *Newsweek*, September 13, 2021, https://www.newsweek.com/jon-voight-champions-larry-elder-replace-gavin-newsom-california-recall-election.

32 Emma Colton, "Former California Democrat Leader Endorses Larry Elder in Campaign Against Gov. Newsom," FOX NEWS, September 14, 2021, https://www.foxnews.com/politics/former-democratic-california-leader-endorses-larry-elder-recall.

Here's how it works. If a candidate agrees to spend no more than $9 million, the California elections officials include a brief bio on each candidate, provided he or she accepts the limitation. Since few candidates can come even close to raising that amount, nearly all opt for the bio. Again, you can raise and spend directly on your campaign as much as you want if you do not accept the limitation—but you don't get the voter pamphlet bio. My campaign leaders insisted that I accept the limit in exchange for the bio. After all, it is not likely, they said, that you will raise more than $9 million. I felt otherwise and said so. Neither Tony Strickland, my cochair, nor Jeff Corless, my campaign manager, thought I could raise that much let alone a lot more. I said, "Guys, I've never run a campaign before, and maybe this is naive, but I have a national show. My listeners love and respect me. If I ask them to contribute money, they'll contribute. I'll blow through that $9 million cap." But I felt that their superior experience topped my green enthusiasm and agreed to the limit.

My campaign won 57 of the 58 counties across the state, losing only San Francisco County—where I did not campaign or spend any advertising money—*by 149 votes.* Over 3.5 million Californians voted for me, many of whom were registered Democrats and Independents who had never voted for a Republican. These voters knew, as I did, that as bad as things were prior to the recall, the Golden State can and should be saved, and not just for the sake of the state, but for the sake of the nation.

My insurgent campaign becomes all the more astonishing when one considers the change in the California electorate from 2003, when Arnold Schwarzenegger won the state's first and only successful gubernatorial recall election, to the electorate I faced in 2021.

Here are the California registered voters in 2003 when Democrat Governor Gray Davis was recalled and replaced by Schwarzenegger:

2003
Registered Dems: 44.1 percent
Registered GOP: 35.3 percent
No Preference: 15.7 percent
Other: 5.0 percent

Here are California registered voters eighteen years later when Newsom faced his recall election:

2021
Registered Dems: 46.5 percent
Registered GOP: 24.1 percent
No Preference: 23.3 percent
Other: 6.2 percent

Registered Democrats increased by almost three percentage points, about 5 percent growth. Registered independents increased by nearly half and, as the *New York Times* noted, California Independents "tend to vote Democratic." Meanwhile, Republicans *decreased* by a whopping one-third!

As to the results of my campaign, and despite this dramatic leftward shift in California's electoral map from 2003 to today, I received almost the exact same percentage of replacement votes as did Schwarzenegger—48.2 percent versus 48.5 percent, respectively.

But after the recall, long-time *Los Angeles Times* columnist George Skelton wrote an "analysis" with the headline: "Newsom's Waning Voter Approval Might've Given the GOP a Shot. But They Blew It in the Recall." He wrote: "Many Democratic voters ignored the contest to replace Newsom if he was recalled, leaving the irrelevant choice mainly to Republicans. And they overwhelmingly preferred the conservative who advocated zero minimum wage, opposed abortion rights, and suggested that descendants of slave owners be paid reparations for loss of their ancestors' property."[33]

In my many rallies and interviews with supporters *no one* asked my views of abortion in this supermajority "pro-choice" state. Ditto for the minimum wage or reparations. My supporters asked what I intended to do about crime, homelessness, and the outrageous cost of a home. But the leftwing media asked about these things. When I replied, "I'm here to discuss crime, homelessness, and that people are leaving California for the first time." The media response? "Elder refuses to answer tough questions."

After the recall election, many pundits, as well as my opponent's campaign manager, pushed the narrative that "Larry Elder was a gift" to Gavin Newsom. A kinder, gentler Republican, they insisted, who distanced himself from the loathsome former president Donald Trump, would have made all the difference in the world, despite the fact that 70 percent of California voters are registered as Democrats or Independents.

---

33 "Newsom's Waning Voter Approval Might've given the GOP a Shot. but They Blew It in the Recall." *Los Angeles Times.* February 18, 2022. https://www.latimes.com/california/story/2022-02-16/skelton-poll-newsom-voter-approval-gop-governor-race-california-recall.

CNN's Lincoln Mitchell wrote: "Elder was precisely what Newsom needed to make the fear of Trumpism real in the eyes of California's substantial Democratic majority. Elder, a long-time conservative talk radio host, is well known among right-wing Californians, but many other voters have only gotten to know him in more recent weeks." A *San Francisco Chronicle* headline read: "Larry Elder Is the Trumpist Who May Save Gavin Newsom's Job."[34]

After the race, *Politico* asserted: "By Labor Day, Newsom had turned what started as an up-or-down vote on his governorship into a choice between him and Elder, the radio show host Newsom relentlessly tethered to Trump...For Newsom, the emergence of Elder as the GOP's standard bearer was an unexpected gift."[35]

Really?

The treatment of Virginia governor Glenn Youngkin and black lieutenant governor Winsome Sears completely destroys the "Elder-was-the-wrong-kind-of-Republican" analysis. The hysterical reaction to the Republican victory demonstrates that any Republican, especially a black one, would have faced the same unhinged attacks leveled against me during my campaign.

After the Republican victory in Virginia, in which Sears—a black, female, Marine veteran with a master's degree—was elected lieutenant governor, black MSNBC pundit Michael

34 Joe Garofoli, "Larry Elder Is the Trumpist that May Save Newsom," *San Francisco Chronicle,* September 12, 2021, https://www.sfchronicle.com/politics/joegarofoli/article/Larry-Elder-is-the-Trumpist-that-may-save-Gavin.

35 David Siders and Carla Marinucci, "How Gavin Newsom Survived the Recall," *POLITICO,* September 15, 2021, https://www.politico.com/news/2021/09/15/how-gavin-newsom-beat-the-recall.

Eric Dyson said: "The problem is, here, they want white supremacy by ventriloquist effect. There is a black mouth moving but a white idea…running on the runway of the tongue of a figure who justifies and legitimates the white supremacist practices."[36]

This was very similar to what was said of me—that because I spoke differently than say, Al Sharpton, I was not "authentically" black.

I did not invite former president Trump to campaign for or with me. Neither did Glenn Youngkin when he ran successfully for governor of Virginia. Like Youngkin, I support school choice, oppose vaccine mandates, and am pro-life. Unlike in the Youngkin race, Trump did *not* publicly endorse me. Still, Newsom described me as "more Trump than Trump." In Newsom's ungracious victory speech, he said: "We may have defeated Trump, but Trumpism is not dead."[37]

About Virginia, CNN's black pundit Van Jones said: "The stakes are high. When this election is over in Virginia, we will know…Have we seen the emergence of the Delta variant of Trumpism? In other words, Youngkin, same disease, but spreads a lot faster and can get to a lot more places."[38]

---

36 Biba Adams, "Dyson on Winsome Sears: 'Black Face Speaking in Behalf of a White Supremacist,'" Yahoo News, November 5, 2021, https://www.yahoo.com/video/dyson-winsome-sears-black-face.

37 Aila Slisco, "Gavin Newsom Warns Trumpism Is Not Dead After Landslide Recall Victory," *Newsweek*, September 15, 2021, https://www.newsweek.com/gavin-newsom-warns-trumpism-not-dead-speech-after-landslide-recall-victory.

38 Khaleda Rahman, "CNN's Van Jones Dubs Glenn Youngkin the 'Delta Variant of Trumpism,'" *Newsweek*, November 3, 2021, https://www.newsweek.com/cnn-van-jones-glenn-youngkin-delta-variant-trumpism.

After Youngkin's victory, Jemele Hill, a black, former ESPN host tweeted: "It's not the messaging, folks. This country simply loves white supremacy."[39] Black MSNBC host Joy Reid said: "You have to be willing to vocalize that these Republicans are dangerous…Stoking that kind of soft white nationalism eventually leads to the hardcore stuff. It leads to the Jan 6 stuff."[40] Soft white nationalism? Black NBC pundit Jason Johnson said: "This was about how white kids feel talking about what black kids go through. Let's just call it what it is."

Virginia Democratic senator Tim Kaine said: "If you look at the Youngkin campaign, they've made it about kind of invented inflated issues like critical race theory…It's unheard of, and it hearkens back to a long tradition in Virginia history."[41] The election of a black, female lieutenant governor, whose Jamaican immigrant father came to America with $1.75 in his pocket, "hearkens back to a long tradition in Virginia history" of Jim Crow segregation?

Black Democratic National Committee Chairman Jaime Harrison said: "This is a dog whistle to divide people…It is about racial divisions, racial hatred, racial animosity…It's sad

---

39 Jemele Hill, Twitter post, November 3, 2021 12:19 a.m., https://twitter.com/jemelehill/status/1455766504650067971?s=20&t=fbMl0_cjTJKcX1b99RihQQ.

40 Daniel Chaitin, "MSNBC Host Joy Reid Says 'Republicans Are Dangerous,'" *Washington Examiner,* November 2, 2021, https://www.washingtonexaminer.com/news/msnbc-host-joy-reid-says-republicans-are-dangerous.

41 Pam Key, "Kaine: Youngkin Campaign 'Hearkens Back' to 'Segregationist Attitudes,'" *Breitbart,* October 31, 2021, https://www.breitbart.com/clips/2021/10/31/kaine-youngkin-campaign-hearkens-back-to-segregationist-attitudes.

to see where the Republican Party is going because they have become a party of fascism and fear."[42]

Don't give me this "Elder was a gift to Newsom" claptrap. This is California, not Virginia. Furthermore, none, repeat *none* of my Republican "Monday Morning" recall rivals chose to run against Newsom in his bid for reelection. Why not? After all, they know "what Elder did wrong." So, why not put those lessons to work?

42 Courtney O'Brien, "DNC Chair Joins Liberals Accusing Youngkin, Critical Race Theory Opponents of Using 'A Racist Dog Whistle,'" FOX NEWS, November 3, 2021, https://www.foxnews.com/media/dnc-chair-youngkin-talking-critical-race-theory-whistle.

Chapter 6

AS GOES CALIFORNIA: THE REAL PROBLEM IS LIBERAL GOVERNANCE

I MADE ABOUT ONE HUNDRED campaign stops across the state during the recall. I was moving constantly—doing radio, TV, and in-person events up and down California. It was like being in a car going ninety miles an hour on the interstate. Nina and I were sitting in a restaurant in the San Jose airport. She noticed a man across the room sitting at the bar wearing a cap that said 'Trump 2024,'" and said "It takes some nerve, in a place this liberal, to wear a cap like that. You should say something to him."

I walked over, tapped him on his shoulder, and complimented him on his headgear.

"Oh, my God!" he said. "Larry Elder, you changed my life! You made me the man I am today."

I invited him to our table where Nate, age forty, energetic, funny and full of life, proceeded to share his life story. His father could neither read nor write but became so successful as a contractor that he employed nearly six hundred people then sold his business and retired at age forty-one. Nate had two siblings and, like me, was the middle child.

Nate had been a promising high school football player but squandered his potential over being angry—at his parents, at the world, just angry. He drank, partied, did drugs, and got kicked out of high school. He enrolled in another, rougher school where he was also a poor student. Then "for some reason," at age sixteen, he began listening to talk radio and my show became his favorite. He heard me talk about my penniless, fatherless dad, who grew up in the Jim Crow South, and whose illiterate, irresponsible mother kicked him out of his house at the age of thirteen, at the beginning of the Great Depression. Nate said he listened daily as I preached hard work, personal responsibility, and insisted that we have a duty, no matter our circumstances, to 'pick up the cards we are dealt and play them to the best of our ability'. He was "inspired" when I insisted that we cannot control the outcome, but we are 100 percent in control of the effort.

Nate had also read my books and columns. On his refrigerator, he had taped my "Personal Pledge 32"—a list of rules to live by that I wrote twenty-five years ago—so that his two children "get a daily reminder to be grateful and stay focused." He now owns a successful contracting business that builds offices and apartment buildings.

Several times during our conversation Nate teared up: "I don't know what I would've done had I not discovered you.

You helped bring me to Christ. And you helped me come to appreciate my father. Now, my dad told me many of the same things you did. But sometimes, you need to hear it from somebody else."

Nate ended our long conversation saying, "Larry, you made my Christmas." He made mine, too.

Sadly, because of California's taxes, regulations and ever-changing COVID-19 mandates for businesses and schools, Nate is leaving. He recently decided to relocate his business and family to Idaho. He was only in San Jose to complete his remaining California projects.

California's loss.

This is a story I hear too often. And I also know something else—all of these problems I faced in my campaign won't stay confined to California—or any other state where the Democratic Party controls the gears of power. Let's take a look at a few other places where Democratic rule has wrecked once great cities.

Chicago has not elected a Republican in a long time. It's the city that gave us Barack Obama and one of the worst mayors who ever lived, in Lori Lightfoot. Chicago crime rates are 67 percent higher than the national average and violent crimes are 143 percent higher. One has a one-in-twenty-six chance of becoming a victim of crime in Chicago. Yet people keep voting Democrats into power.

In very liberal Wayne County, Michigan, where Detroit is located, 68.3 percent of the people voted Democrat in the last presidential election, with 30.3 percent voting Republican, and the remaining 1.4 percent voting Independent. Wayne County has voted Democrat in every presidential election since 2000. Detroit City, 82.7 percent black, has a median household income of $26,000. There are over one hundred thousand empty properties, and nearly 40 percent of people there live in poverty. The neighborhood south of 8 Mile Road (the street made famous by rapper Eminem's hit movie) has one of the highest murder rates in the country. Kwame Kilpatrick was mayor of Detroit from 2002 to 2008. In March 2013, he was convicted on twenty-four federal felony counts and sentenced to twenty-eight years in federal prison. In January 2021, President Donald Trump commuted his sentence.

Philadelphia is the largest city in the Commonwealth of Pennsylvania and the sixth most populous city in the United States. Philly district attorney Seth Williams served almost three years in federal prison and was released in April 2020. In 2016, US representative Chaka Fattah was sentenced to ten years in prison for stealing hundreds of thousands in public funds to repay an illegal campaign loan, accepting bribes, and using campaign cash to pay off part of his son's college tuition debt. In November 2021, Philadelphia's high-profile, politically influential labor leader of IBEW (International Brotherhood of Electrical Workers) Local 98, John "Johnny Doc" Dougherty, was convicted in his federal bribery trial. His pal, city councilman Bobby Henon, received sports tickets worth $11,807 from Dougherty and a "stream of personal benefits" that federal prosecutors said Henon knew were in exchange for his "performance of official acts at the direction of and on behalf of" the union chief. Henon was elected to the city council in 2011 and reelected to his third term in 2019, serving as majority leader in his second term after a unanimous vote electing him from 2016–2019. In January 2022, two months after Henon was convicted of bribery and conspiracy, Henon finally resigned. Both men faced up to twenty years in prison for the most serious charges.

And then there's Baltimore.

Marilyn Mosby, the city's top prosecutor since 2015, was indicted in January 2022 on federal charges of perjury and filing false mortgage applications related to her purchase of two Florida vacation homes. She was accused of twice falsely claiming work-related financial hardship from COVID-19 in order to withdraw $90,000 from her city employee retirement account. Baltimore homicides surpassed three hundred in 2021, in line with the two previous years, and the number of nonfatal shootings more than doubled the homicide number.

The nation got to know Mosby during the troubles over Freddie Gray, a black man who died in police custody after resisting arrest. Mosby helped turn this tragedy into a racism thing, in a city that's 45 percent black. The city council is 100 percent Democrat and the majority of them are black. Nick J. Mosby, president of the Baltimore City Council, is Marilyn's husband. The top cop at the time was black, the number-two cop was black, and the majority of the command staff black. The mayor was black. The attorney general was black, and yet the incident turned into riots over racism. The charge is absurd, so I won't dwell on it.

How about a look at Baltimore education? Educational assessments from the program iReady of 628 students at Patterson High School in early 2022 found some students doing so poorly that they tested at a kindergarten level. Seventy-one Patterson students were reading at a kindergarten level, and eighty-eight were reading at a first-grade level.

Only twelve students—just 1.9 percent—read at grade level. And we thought it was bad in Los Angeles! Philadelphia's last Republican mayor was Bernard Samuel in 1948.

Famous for its Gateway Arch, the problems of the county of St. Louis increased even more in 2014, after the police shooting of Michael Brown in Ferguson erupted in weeks of unrest. (Police were later vindicated.) A plan known as "Better Together" was created by local leaders and heavily funded by local billionaire Rex Sinquefield. The idea was to combine St. Louis city and county and merge their governments, in an effort to lift the economically ailing city. The plan fell apart.

The city was back in the news when a St. Louis couple, Mark and Patricia McCloskey, stood outside their home and brandished guns at protesters who had broken a metal gate to enter their gated community and were threatening them on a private street outside their home. President Trump spoke out in defense of the McCloskeys, whose law licenses in the state had been suspended. They later spoke at the Republican National Convention and were pardoned by Mike Parson, the governor of Missouri. Mark McCloskey later announced a Senate run for the seat then held by retiring Republican Roy Blunt. Meanwhile, Tishaura Oneda Jones, who served from 2008 to 2013 in the Missouri House of Representatives and as treasurer of St. Louis from 2013 to 2021, was elected mayor in 2021. She is the first black woman to hold the position.

The last Republican mayor of St. Louis was Aloys P. Kaufmann in 1949. In 2019, June Hamilton-Dean, a Democrat, former city councilmember and community development director was found guilty of felony counts of forgery and public misconduct. Her brother, Oliver Hamilton, was sentenced to sixty months in prison for using taxpayer funds to make personal purchases while he was East St. Louis Township supervisor. In September 2021, the highly political St. Louis-Kansas City Carpenters Regional Council, a twenty thousand-plus-member construction union, dissolved and reassigned authority to the Chicago Regional Council of Carpenters. The council had been led since 2015 by Executive Secretary-Treasurer Al Bond, a major donor to local candidates and controversial causes like the failed proposed merger of St. Louis and St. Louis County. The United Brotherhood of Carpenters had been under a federal investigation following the 2019 indictment of George Laufenberg, who controlled funds for the New Jersey Carpenters Pension, Annuity, Health and Training/Apprenticeship and was a former commissioner of the Port Authority of New York and New Jersey. The *St. Louis Post-Dispatch* was told by "people with ties to the union and the labor movement" that Bond in St. Louis was removed as leader of the local, but was not told why.

On February 8, 2022, the *New York Post* reported: "Nearly every single [New York] city police precinct has seen spikes in crime so far this year—including five in which the rate has doubled, according to the latest troubling NYPD statistics."[43] Seventy-two out of the city's seventy-seven police precincts saw crime increase. One Brooklyn cop suggested: "At this rate, we will lose the city by St. Patrick's Day." And the only precinct in Manhattan that did not see an increase in crime

43 Larry Celona, Steven Vago, and Jorge Fitz-Gibbon, "'No Neighborhood Is Safe,' Crime Up in Nearly Every NYC Precinct: Latest Stats," *New York Post*, February 8, 2022, https://nypost.com/2022/02/08/crime-up-in-nearly-every-single-nyc-precinct-stats-show.

rate was the 22nd Precinct, the one covering Central Park. Another policeman said: "Only the squirrels are safe. Tourists will never come back."

What does it all add up to? With one-party rule by Democrats in any major American city, one sees multigenerational chaos, criminality, and a dumbed-down government school system.

California has had Republican leaders in recent years. Republican Pete Wilson left office in 1999, and Republican Arnold Schwarzenegger left office in 2011. The last Republican mayor of Los Angeles was Richard J. Riordan who left office July 1, 2001. The last Republican mayor of San Francisco was George Christopher who left office January 7, 1964.

But in November 2016, California Democrats recaptured a two-thirds supermajority in both houses of the Legislature. This gave them the ability to pass taxes, amend political spending laws, put constitutional amendments on the ballot, or quickly implement any legislation—without any Republican support. That year, for the twelfth year in a row, California ranked dead last in *Chief Executive* magazine's annual "Best and Worst States for Business" survey of 513 CEOs from across the nation. In 2021, California was still dead last.

More facts about one-party California:

1. The state's sales tax was the highest in the nation in 2021 at 7.25 percent.
2. Thanks to the 2012 passage of Proposition 30 and, in 2016, of Proposition 55, California now has the top state income tax rate at 13.3 percent.

3. A September 2017 report by the nonprofit Truth in Accounting ranked states by taxpayer burden, which they define as the amount each state taxpayer would have had to send to their state's treasury in 2016 to erase the state's debt. For California, that amount was $21,600. Other states were higher, such as Illinois with $50,400 per person, but California is different. As of 2020, it had a $3 trillion gross state product (GSP). In other words, if it were a sovereign nation its economy would rank as the world's fifth largest, ahead of the United Kingdom and just behind Germany. So why is the state so wrapped in debt?
4. According to the Public Policy Institute of California, more than a third of Californians live on or near the poverty line. In 2018, California had the highest poverty rate in the United States.
5. According to the Milken Institute, California is falling behind national COVID-19 recovery efforts. The state's weekly unemployment claims make up almost 20 percent of the United States' new claims, even though the state supplies roughly 12 percent of the national workforce.
6. According to a ranking of "Electric Sales, Revenue, and Average Price" from the US Energy Information Administration, California ranks forty-second out of fifty states in annual average price per kilowatt-hour.
7. In 2016, California, the nation's leading agricultural state, passed a law targeting greenhouse gases produced by dairy cows and other livestock. That's right, the Golden State now has a law regulating cow emissions.

8. As of 2018, more than a million undocumented immigrants had received California driver's licenses, which is all you need to vote (if you're even asked for identification in California).
9. According to FireScience.org, California ranks number one in state wildfires, with 87,742 acres burned since 2002. (Hey, we're number one in something!)
10. In 2018, a study by *U.S. News* ranked "quality of life" for residents of every state, taking into account each state's "air quality, pollution, voter participation, social support and more." California came in dead last, following New Jersey at forty-ninth and Indiana at forty eighth.

Those are just a few examples. Google the term "Reasons Why California Sucks"—and stand back.

Bestselling author Michael Shellenberger is founder and president of Environmental Progress, an independent, nonpartisan research organization based in Berkeley, California. A fearless truthteller, Shellenberger wrote the book *SanFranSicko: Why Progressives Ruin Cities.*

"I moved out to San Francisco when I was a young radical to work on political causes. And while I still support a lot of that work, it just went too far," said Shellenberger in a YouTube channel interview with libertarian John Stossel.[44]

Shellenberger noted a thief can go into a drugstore and steal $950 worth of items and nobody will do anything because of Proposition 47. Stossel played a clip from the swearing-in

44 John Stossel, "Why Progressives Ruin Cities," YouTube, January 25, 2022, https://www.youtube.com/watch?v=IHXtHZpDvAo.

ceremony of San Francisco district attorney Chesa Boudin, who angrily told his audience: "Join us in rejecting the notion that to be free, we must cage others." Boudin, of course, would know all about that: His parents were members of the terrorist group the Weather Underground and were arrested on murder charges when he was a baby. He would be raised by other members of the group, including Bill Ayers.

Prop 47 was sold to the public with explainer videos like the one that promised, "Instead of investing in prisons, Proposition 47 will divert $1 billion to K–12 education, mental health and drug treatment programs."

Stossel then showed Jay-Z on a stage talking about the importance of Prop 47.

Another video showed a young, black male, in a store aisle with a bicycle, filling a large garbage bag while a security guard and female employee stood by watching. Stossel said, "Knowing they won't be jailed, thieves steal right in front of security guards."

Yet another clip showed San Francisco streets filled with tent cities where drug users lit up in public, confident no one would interfere. This was followed by a video of a middle-aged homeless woman, sitting on the streets of San Francisco smoking crack every day for twelve years. She boasted about the ease of buying and using drugs in the city. The woman said she was from San Jose, where similar behavior would get her locked up. Even she complained that San Francisco should do something.

Shellenberger said other cities, particularly rich ones like Carmel, didn't let people use drugs in public and built a sufficient number of homeless shelters. San Francisco activists, said Stossel, made the case that "everybody has the right to their own apartment." Shellenberger called the argument, "Completely crazy because it costs $750,000 to build a single unit apartment in San Francisco. Homelessness is just a function of whether or not you allow people to camp in public or not." What, said Stossel, about one's right to be outdoors without being forced off the street, assuming they aren't directly threatening anybody? Shellenberger countered: "We should defend those rights because that's part of our freedom. But you don't have a right to shoot heroin at the public park."

In San Francisco, an average of seventy-four cars are broken into every day, often by drug users seeking to pay for their addictions. Shellenberger said San Francisco officials he talked to about this were both defensive and embarrassed. "They don't know what to do because there's a very powerful progressive constituency that insists that people who are categorized as victims should not have to follow the law. I was a progressive activist for a very long time and only recently in researching this book did I decide I couldn't use that label anymore. Progressivism has become the abdication of personal responsibility."

Even San Francisco mayor London Breed was changing her progressive tune. Stossel played a video where she said, "It's time that the reign of criminals who are destroying our city, it is time for it to come to an end." San Francisco's policing, she promised, would be more aggressive, "and less tolerant of all the bullshit that has destroyed our city."

When running, I received letters from convicts—convicts!—concerned about the deterioration of the state. I also spoke to my friend Chico Brown. Originally from Compton,

California, Chico, a former gang member, went to prison for drug dealing. He got shot in 1976. He joined the Crips. His best friend died in his arms at age fifteen. His own mother didn't know what he was doing until he went to prison. I met him right before he went to prison on the old Geraldo Rivera daily talk show. The episode was about the lengthy sentences that people like Chico faced for dealing cocaine. I was the only one of the "community leaders" who said no matter how you feel about these laws, Chico knew the consequences and should do the time. The studio erupted with anger. Chico and the other panelists fumed.

When Chico got out of prison, he called my radio show. Here's what our conversation sounded like:

> **Chico:** "Remember me? I met you on the Geraldo show a few years ago."
>
> **Elder:** "I do. Last we talked you weren't exactly pleased with me."
>
> **Chico:** "I wasn't. You were the only one up there who said, 'You should go to jail.' And nearly every day I was in prison, I promised to get out, track your butt down—and kill you. But little by little, I realized, hey, you were the only one telling me to 'take responsibility.' When I got out, I became a counselor with an inner-city nonprofit youth center called A Place Called Home, where I encourage kids not to take the same path I did. And I just called to say, 'Thank you for stopping me from thinking that I was a victim and that the

world owed me something. I'm not, and no one owes me anything.' It is, as you said then, about decisions."

I got his number. We had dinner and have been friends ever since. Today, he's involved in developing entertainment properties. He became a community activist and youth sports organizer and now raises money for A Place Called Home. He enthusiastically endorsed my candidacy.

About today's increase in violent crime in California cities, Chico says: "It was definitely political for me. In the city of Compton, I formed a pact with Crips and Pirus (a black gang based in Compton that later became the Bloods) to stop all the gang violence in the city. I had a program that started off with four Crips and four Bloods. At the end of the day, I was meeting with three thousand Crips and Pirus. So, I witnessed in front of the city council, which is all Democrats. They denied my program. I was doing a television show about this program backed by Mark Wahlberg and Penny Marshall. It went viral because nobody could believe why they stopped this program. And at the time, there was not one murder in the city of Compton in the year I did that. The program ended up breaking up, and now Compton is the worst ever. Compton provided no funding. Parks and recreation were down. They didn't help kids get jobs. I focused on construction, hired ten Crips and ten Bloods to ease the problem because the city wouldn't help us. Once the city denied me, all the issues with gang-banging started back because these kids didn't have life skills, no training, and that's why I was helping these kids get with common construction so they could get jobs. Once the program stopped, they went back to doing what they know best, and that's gang banging, selling drugs, and going to prison."

Chico says with the right kind of commitment and leadership the crime problem would improve. But, at the end of the day, he said, crime is a choice. And if people feel they can get away with it, crime will go up.

After another recent on-air interview with Chico, I got a call from a trucker, an ex-convict convicted of three felonies, who did his sentence in the Los Angeles County jail. The trucker eventually had his record expunged. He said my discussion with Chico resonated with him and he called to thank me for helping people turn their lives around by telling them to "take charge of their own lives and to not play the victim."

It was that attitude that drove my positions on the pandemic. Throughout my campaign, I talked about the mandates for face masks and mandates for vaccines, which I promised to repeal. I said I was not "anti-vax," but as a member of a "high-risk group" because of my age and a rare blood condition, I had a "comorbidity." Mandates are an entirely different matter. I reminded them that both Joe Biden and Kamala Harris had expressed vaccine hesitancy. For instance, during a debate, Harris said if Donald Trump told her to take the vaccine, she wasn't going to take it. And now those who support mandates are supposedly shocked that people follow their advice. Such hypocrisy. "The decision," I said, "should be an individual choice."

This was, of course, at odds with Newsom's policies, widely acknowledged as the most extreme in the country. By February 2022, four US states—Connecticut, Delaware,

New Jersey, and Oregon, predominantly blue states—decided to cut back the mandates. Meanwhile, California remained one of thirteen states to retain a mask mandate in schools. California's universal mask mandate required residents to wear face coverings in all indoor public spaces and in indoor common areas of outdoor "mega-events" with five thousand or more people, regardless of vaccination status. Los Angeles County also required all people attending large indoor and outdoor events to wear masks except when eating and drinking. So mask mandates were in effect at the 2022 NFL conference championship game in Los Angeles unless fans in attendance, including the Los Angeles mayor Eric Garcetti, chose to ignore the mandates and appear mask-less. Not to worry, said Garcetti: "I wore my mask the entire game. When people ask for a photograph, I hold my breath and put in here and people can see that. There is a 0 percent chance of infection from that."[45]

Mask mandates were in effect weeks later at the Los Angeles Superbowl, though many fans in attendance chose not to wear them, with the majority cheering on the teams while not wearing masks.

Fortunately, there were no mass arrests.

California's mask mandate for fully vaccinated people ended in mid-February 2022, but mandates remained for school staff and students. This caused protests across the state when school districts began sending home unmasked students. California Health and Human Services secretary Dr.

---

45 Joseph Gedeon, "Garcetti Defends Maskless Photo at NFL Game: 'I Hold My Breath,'" *POLITICO*, February 3, 2022, https://www.politico.com/news/2022/02/03/los-angeles-mayor-garcetti-maskless-photo-00005284.

Mark Ghaly promised to review student vaccination rates, COVID-19 numbers, hospitalizations, and other trends. The California Small School Districts' Association, which represents six hundred school districts and charter schools, said many rural schools were already dropping the mandates.

At some point, even liberals rebel. And for Californians, this sometimes just means leaving.

Chapter 7

"THE BLACK FACE OF WHITE SUPREMACY"

IT'S INCREDIBLE HOW MUCH FALSE media narratives warp people's worldviews. Thomas Sowell once said that "liberals seem to assume that, if you don't believe in their particular political solutions, then you don't really care about the people that they claim to want to help." For many on the left, disagreement means "you're a bad person."

Mainstream media outlets enforce these beliefs daily, to the point that for most people it becomes difficult to see otherwise—unless reality whacks them in the face.

That's my job, and sometimes it happens in the strangest ways.

After two back surgeries, the last one not so successful, I suffer from sciatica on the right side of my body. A friend recommended a massage therapist named Jackie.

Jackie's "office" was her home in a nice area of Los Angeles in the San Fernando Valley. When she opened the door, I was punched in the face by a blast of marijuana.

"I hope this doesn't bother you," she said.

"Not if you can do something about my sciatica," I responded.

There might've been two or three inches on Jackie's face, neck, shoulders, and arms where there were no tattoos. I've never seen anyone with so many face rings, earrings, nose rings, and rings on every finger, including the thumbs.

While she worked on me as I lay face down on her massage table in her big living room, Motown music played.

"Wow," I said. "I haven't heard that Marvin Gaye song in years." I told her how much I loved Motown, as well as music of that period including Stax record stars like Otis Redding. I told her that I'd actually had a tour of the Motown studios on W. Grand Boulevard in Detroit when I was about ten years old. We talked about how Marvin Gaye died, shot by his own father, on Gage Avenue, not blocks from where I lived in South Central Los Angeles.

When a Temptations song came on, I told her about the careers and fate of the "original" five members, and that Smokey Robinson wrote their signature hit "My Girl," which I played at my wedding nearly thirty years ago. "This is fascinating," Jackie said. "I didn't know any of this."

Jackie, a white woman approximately forty years old, told me that she married a black man and that's how she acquired her appreciation for "black music." They had adopted a black child, who walked in as his mom worked on me. He was a teenager, a very good basketball player, and an excellent student, and Jackie hoped that he would get a scholarship to play high-level basketball in college. He was polite and charming, and we chatted for a few minutes. I asked her son about his plans after graduating from high school; Jackie answered for him. When I asked him where he planned on going to college, Jackie again answered for him.

Finally I said, "Is your son allowed to speak for himself?" Jackie stopped interrupting, and her son came across as thoughtful, poised, and polite. When he left, I told Jackie, "Impressive young man. Good job, Mom."

Jackie said she and her husband broke up several years ago and that she essentially raised her son by herself because his dad was "in and out his life" and frequently failed to pay child support. We talked about what I called "the number one problem" in America, "particularly in the black community"—that so many kids are raised without fathers in the home. Jackie agreed wholeheartedly.

Then Jackie said, "You know that I know who you are, don't you? I knew you ran for governor when someone called to make the appointment for you. I just didn't want to say anything because I disagree with your politics. But had I known what a nice guy you are, and what a great sense of humor you have, I would've voted for you. You should've shown more personality when you were running."

I asked her whether she had attended any of my rallies during the campaign. She had not. "You know," I said, "at every political rally, I cracked several jokes, made fun of myself, and ended virtually all my rallies with another joke. Yet in all my television coverage, and all the articles written about the campaign with few exceptions, they never talked about the jokes, the laughter, and how people at the rally not only heard about serious issues and what I would do about them, but they also had a good time. The news covered me like I was the Grim Reaper."

Then I asked, "Do you have any Republican friends?"

"No."

"Do you have any friends you would describe as conservative?"

"No."

I told her: "One of my closest friends is named Allen. I attended his wedding and liked his wife very much. They have two children. When the kids were young Allen got divorced. His ex, Penny, got custody of the kids. I maintained a good relationship with Penny, but she would denigrate Allen to the kids. Not too surprisingly they learned to resent Allen, even though Allen readily paid child support and was actively involved in his kids' lives. That they resented Allen hurt him very deeply. We spent hours talking about this. I told him to just keep being the best father he could and, eventually, the kids would realize that there are two sides to every story and that their mom's attitude toward Allen need not be their own. Well, it took a few years, but now Allen and his kids are very close and they appreciate everything he's done and continues to do for them.

"I tell you all of this because if all my friends were liberal and if all I watched and read came from liberal sources, I'd dislike Trump, Republicans, and conservatives, too. The *New York Times*, the country's most influential newspaper, has not endorsed a Republican for president since 1956. The *Washington Post*, the second most influential newspaper, has *never* endorsed a Republican for president.

"And liberal reporters who daily cover the White House outnumber the Republican/conservative reporters twelve to one. I kid you not!

"You know, most of my Republican friends have a good sense of humor. Most of them are pretty sensitive, and most, like you, have raised children while dealing with many of the same challenges. I don't know any who don't give to charity, some very generously."

"Jackie," I smiled, "you should get out more."

When I came back two weeks later, Jackie said that she had told her neighbors about our conversation. None voted for me, she said, and one called me a "racist S.O.B." When Jackie asked "what makes Larry a 'racist?'" she said they had no example. When she told them I was "a really nice guy," Jackie said "they did not want to hear it."

"Gee," I said. "Kind of like you two weeks ago."

She laughed.

"Welcome to my world, Jackie."

A great deal of what the mainstream media puts out as reasoned thought or even "common knowledge" is propaganda designed to keep people in the dark about the truth. I've run up against this problem for years as a commentator, but it hit me in a completely different way during the campaign.

For instance, I was asked about abortion over and over as if it had anything to do with why Newsom was facing a recall election. Again, the California legislature is two-thirds Democrat. They're "pro-choice." Were I elected governor of California, there would be zero chance that lawmakers would put a bill on my desk restricting abortion.

I asked reporters who interviewed me during the campaign to ask Newsom at what point during a pregnancy does he believe an abortion should be illegal?

On my show, I often play a quote from the late Justice Antonin Scalia. During an interview, he was asked about abortion. He said law school taught him nothing about abortion or about doctor-assisted suicide. These are issues, he said, that shouldn't be before the courts. They should be left to the democratic process.

Similarly, I was continually asked about minimum wage again, as if this had anything to do with the recall. I had written and said many times the ideal minimum wage should be zero. The media interpreted that to mean "Elder wants people to be paid nothing."

The lack of understanding of economics in the progressive media is astonishing. When the NFL playoffs were going on, I was watching Cleveland lose yet again to the Pittsburgh Steelers. During halftime, the NFL showed one of these feel-good, pro-black public service announcements. A young black man came on and said when he got a job as a black man, he would make $10,000 less per year than a similarly qualified white person.

What? Like that's a rule throughout our society?

I went on the air the next morning and played the clip. I said, "Let's just think this through. You're an employer. You can hire a black person at ten grand less, and he'll be equally productive? What do you do? Well, I'd call in all the white people en masse, fire them, hire black people, and pocket the difference."

Furthermore, I said that the lesser salary claim is an inconsistent argument. On the one hand, it implied employers are so racist they're willing to overpay a white person rather than hire a qualified black person. On the other hand, the same employer must have a minimum wage in place because the employee was being underpaid in order for the employer to make more money. It's a completely inconsistent argument.

During a conversation with a reporter from Los Angeles's Fox 11 News, she asked me about minimum wage. I told her a *New York Times* editorial in 1987 said the ideal minimum wage was $0.00. They made all the arguments I had made. By setting a minimum wage, you're pricing unskilled people out of work, and the people that are most disproportionately hurt are black. The next victims are women who are secondary and tertiary wage earners.

Famed economist Milton Friedman once said, "The minimum wage law is the most anti-Negro law on our statute books."[46] The market should set the rate, just as the states should rule on abortion or not abortion.

Speaking to the Fox 11 reporter, I asked, "Have you ever studied economics?"

"Yes," she said.

"Who's your favorite economist?" I asked. She was silent. "You don't know?" I asked. She hesitated. "Okay, name an economist," I said. She couldn't. "Do you know who Adam Smith

46 Mark J. Perry, "Milton Friedman in a 1966 Newsweek Op-ed: The Minimum-wage Law Is a "Monument to the Power of Superficial Thinking,"" *AEI*, December 5, 2016, https://www.aei.org/carpe-diem/milton-friedman-in-a-1966-newsweek-op-ed-the-minimum-wage-law-is-a-monument-to-the-power-of-superficial-thinking.

was?" I asked, referring to the father of modern economics. "You never heard of him?"

"No."

"Have you ever heard of Milton Friedman?"

"No."

"You don't know any economists?"

"The person that taught my course in college."

"What is his or her name?"

She didn't remember.

Nor did she know Paul Krugman, the liberal economist and columnist for the *New York Times*, who once considered minimum wage harmful. Apparently, she doesn't read the *New York Times.* When the Fox affiliate played the interview on TV and posted a lengthier excerpt online, they took out our exchange about economists.

I got the worst treatment from black media and black writers. In an interview during the recall, Tavis Smiley, formerly with NPR and PBS, called me "antiblack."

"Tavis, what makes me antiblack?" I asked.

"Well, you're against reparations," Tavis said.

"Barack Obama was against reparations, was he antiblack?"

About twelve years ago, Tavis, with left-wing Professor Cornel West, were guests on my radio show.[47] Here's some of our exchange:

"Here's what I find, Tavis, about your analysis. I know you're not a fan of Ronald Reagan. You once said that Ronald Reagan, quote, 'tortured blacks.' Ronald Reagan did not have

---

47 Sean Giodano, "Larry Elder Hosts Tavis Smiley and Cornel West," YouTube, December 1, 2019, https://www.youtube.com/watch?v=uYUMbZKhZ7s.

a specific black-jobs agenda. What he did was cut taxes very deeply. He slowed down the rate of government spending and he continued and accelerated deregulation policies that were started by Jimmy Carter. The black adult unemployment rate fell faster than the white adult unemployment rate. The black teenage unemployment rate fell far faster than did the white teenage unemployment rate. Black businesses were created at a faster rate. The revenues grew at a faster rate. All because Ronald Reagan dramatically cut taxes and dramatically reduced the rate of government regulation.

"The Obama administration did the opposite. He's spent money. He's taxed. He's threatening to increase taxes even more. He's imposed billions of dollars in regulations. And fast forward to two years in office, we got 9.1 percent unemployment. And during the Reagan era, Tavis, unemployment, in fact, was even higher than the highest during this great recession. So, I don't understand why it is that you don't say the agenda ought to be what Ronald Reagan did."

Here's Tavis's response: "The short answer is this. You're awfully good at this. You've been doing it for seventeen years. Nice try. Ronald Reagan decimated this country. I don't know what America you were living in, respectfully. He decimated America."

My turn. "Decimated? In what way?"

Tavis said Reagan did it in "every way"—just a rotten generality. He kept at it with the angry accusations. "The one thing that Ronald Reagan did for people of color was to support the earned income tax credit, but every other stat you cited we just don't have time on radio to go number for number. Every stat you cited, vis-à-vis people of color, does not measure up when you talk to the people of color who had to live through the hell of those eight years of Ronald Reagan."

I wanted to know more about this so-called hell. "What do you mean, 'talk to the people?' I've just given you labor stats and census stats. These are facts, Tavis. Unemployment fell faster for the black community than in the white community, it fell faster for teens, it fell faster for adults, fell faster for Hispanics. Now you're telling me when you talk to these people—"

"It's not true," he interrupted with a generalized objection, a typical liberal tactic.

I kept on. "They don't like Reagan, so therefore, facts go out the window?"

More of the same came. "Your numbers are not true. When I get back to my office later today or tomorrow, I'll send you some more numbers. You know this, numbers don't lie, but people do."

I smiled, "You're calling me a liar, aren't you, Tavis? You want to take this outside?"

He laughed, but I'm still waiting for Tavis's "correct" numbers.

Democrats talk a big game about fair, reasoned debates. President Joe Biden, during the 2020 campaign said things like we need to "restore civility." A 2020 Biden campaign ad described the election as an "opportunity to leave the dark, angry politics of the past behind us." After Biden's election, he, Democrats, and the media urged a "return to civility."

But when did the Democrats practice the very civility to which they seek to return? To the contrary, they have been comparing Republicans to Nazis since at least the 1960s. It was always a crude tactic and has only gotten cruder over time.

Let's go to the videotape.

When Barry Goldwater accepted the 1964 Republican nomination, California's Democratic governor Pat Brown said, "The stench of fascism is in the air."[48]

Former representative William Clay Sr., D-Missouri, said President Ronald Reagan was "trying to replace the Bill of Rights with fascist precepts lifted verbatim from *Mein Kampf*."[49]

Coretta Scott King, in 1980, said, "I am scared that if Ronald Reagan gets into office, we are going to see more of the Ku Klux Klan and a resurgence of the Nazi Party."

After Republicans took control of the House in the mid-'90s, Representative John Dingell, D-Michigan, compared the newly conservative-majority House to "the Duma and the Reichstag," referring to the legislature set up by Czar Nicholas II of Russia and the parliament of the German Weimar Republic that brought Hitler to power.

About President George Herbert Walker Bush, Representative Maxine Waters, D-California, said: "I believe [Bush] is a racist for many, many reasons...[He's] a mean-spirited man who has no care or concern about what happens to the African American community...I truly believe that."[50]

---

48 Rick Perlstein, "How the 1964 Republican Convention Sparked a Revolution from the Right," *Smithsonian* Magazine, August 2008, https://www.smithsonianmag.com/history/1964-republican-convention-revolution-from-the-right.

49 Christopher Tremoglie, "A 50-Year History of the Worst Comparison," *National Review*, June 21, 2019, https://www.nationalreview.com/corner/a-50-year-history-of-the-worst-comparison.

50 "Rep. Waters Labels Bush 'a Racist,' Endorses Clinton." *Los Angeles Times*. July 9, 1992. https://www.latimes.com/archives/la-xpm-1992-07-09-mn-2366-story.html..

About the Republican-controlled House, longtime Harlem Democratic Representative Charlie Rangel said in 1994: "It's not 's---' or 'n-----' anymore. [Republicans] say, 'Let's cut taxes.'" A decade later, Rangel said, "George [W.] Bush is our Bull Connor," referring to the Birmingham, Alabama segregationist superintendent of public safety who sicced dogs and turned fire hoses on civil rights workers. Rangel missed the irony that Connor was in fact a Democrat.

Donna Brazile, Al Gore's presidential campaign manager, said in 1999: "Republicans have a white boy attitude, [which means] 'I must exclude, denigrate and leave behind.' They don't see it or think about it. It's a culture."

The following year, Brazile said: "The Republicans bring out Colin Powell and [Representative] J. C. Watts, [R-Oklahoma], because they have no program, no policy...They'd rather take pictures with black children than feed them." In 2001, feminist superlawyer Gloria Allred referred to Colin Powell and Condoleezza Rice as "Uncle Tom types."

About President George W. Bush, former vice president Al Gore said: "[Bush's] executive branch has made it a practice to try and control and intimidate news organizations, from PBS to CBS to *Newsweek*...And every day, they unleash squadrons of digital brownshirts to harass and hector any journalist who is critical of the President."

"Digital brownshirts?"

About President George W. Bush, George Soros, the billionaire Democratic donor, said: "The Bush administration and the Nazi and communist regimes all engaged in the politics of fear...Indeed, the Bush administration has been able to improve on the techniques used by the Nazi and communist propaganda machines."

Former NAACP chairman Julian Bond, in a 2006 speech at historically black Fayetteville State University, said, "The Republican Party would have the American flag and the swastika flying side by side."

Former Vermont governor Howard Dean, chairman of the Democratic National Committee in 2005, described the contest between Democrats and Republicans as "a struggle between good and evil. And we're the good." Three years later, Dean referred to the GOP as "the white party."

After Hurricane Katrina, Democratic Missouri Senate candidate Claire McCaskill said President George W. Bush "let people die on rooftops in New Orleans because they were poor and because they were black." Then representative Barney Frank, D-Massachusetts, opined that Bush's administration engaged in "ethnic cleansing by inaction...So by simply not doing anything to alleviate this...they let the hurricane do the ethnic cleansing, and their hands are clean."

In 2006, then senator Hillary Clinton said, "The [Republican-controlled] House of Representatives...has been run like a plantation. And you know what I'm talking about."[51]

Debbie Wasserman Schultz, Democratic National Committee chairwoman in 2011, said "Republicans...want to literally drag us all the way back to Jim Crow laws."[52]

---

51 Clarence Page, "Plantation Politics Revisited, Again," *Chicago Tribune*, January 21, 2006, https://www.chicagotribune.com/news/ct-xpm-2006-01-22-0601220266-story.html.

52 John McCormack, "DNC Chair: Republicans Want to 'Literally Drag Us All the Way Back to Jim Crow Laws,'" *Washington Examiner*, June 6, 2011, https://www.washingtonexaminer.com/weekly-standard/dnc-chair-republicans-want-to-literally-drag-us-all-the-way-back-to-jim-crow-laws.

Left-wing actor/singer and activist Harry Belafonte, who marched with close friend Dr. Martin Luther King Jr., called President George W. Bush a racist. When asked whether the number and prominence of blacks in the Bush administration perhaps suggested a lack of racism, Belafonte explained, "Hitler had a lot of Jews high up in the hierarchy of the Third Reich."[53]

Then representative Keith Ellison, D-Minnesota, former vice chairman of the Democratic National Committee and now the Minnesota attorney general, compared President George W. Bush and 9/11 to Adolf Hitler and the destruction of the Reichstag, the German parliament building: "9/11 is the juggernaut in American history and it allows...it's almost like, you know, the Reichstag fire," Ellison said. "After the Reichstag was burned, they blamed the Communists for it, and it put the leader of that country [Hitler] in a position where he could basically have authority to do whatever he wanted."[54]

Former representative Jim McDermott, D-Washington, said in 2002: "What we are dealing with right now in this country is whether we are having a kind of bloodless, silent coup... President [George W. Bush] is trying to bring to himself all the power to become an emperor—to create Empire America."

Then governor Scott Walker, a Wisconsin Republican who dared to rein in excessive public employee compensation

---

53 David S. Wyman Institute for Holocaust Studies, "Author of Holocaust Book Cited by Harry Belafonte Criticizes Belafonte," History News Network, August 11, 2005, https://historynewsnetwork.org/article/14001.

54 Washington Free Beacon Staff, "FLASHBACK: In 2007, Keith Ellison Compared 9-11 Attacks to Reichstag Fire," *Washington Free Beacon*, November 16, 2016, https://freebeacon.com/politics/flashback-2007-ellison-compared-911-attacks-reichstag-fire.

packages, received the full Nazi treatment. The hard-left blog *Libcom.org* posted in 2011: "Scott Walker is a fascist, perhaps not in the classical sense since he doesn't operate in the streets, but a fascist nonetheless...He is a fascist, for his program takes immediate and direct aim at [a sector of] the working class."

After the 2012 Republican National Convention and the nomination of former Massachusetts governor Mitt Romney, then California Democratic Party chairman John Burton said, "[Republicans] lie, and they don't care if people think they lie. As long as you lie, [Nazi propaganda minister] Joseph Goebbels—the big lie—you keep repeating it."

Dick Harpootlian, the then chairman of the South Carolina Democratic Party in 2012, compared the state's Republican governor to Hitler's mistress. When told that the Republicans were holding a competing press conference at a NASCAR Hall of Fame basement studio, Harpootlian told the South Carolina delegation: "[Gov. Nikki Haley] was down in the bunker, à la Eva Braun."

During the 2012 presidential race, then-vice president Joe Biden told a heavily black audience that candidate Mitt Romney, accused of opposing more Wall Street regulation, is "gonna put y'all back in chains."

In 2014, Representative Charlie Rangel—as seen previously—has been pushing the same line for decades—said, "Some [Republicans] believe that slavery isn't over, and they think they won the Civil War."

And, during the 2016 presidential campaign, Hillary Clinton famously said: "You know, to just be grossly generalistic, you could put half of Trump's supporters into what I call the basket of deplorables. Right? The racist, sexist, homophobic, xenophobic, Islamophobic—you name it. And unfortunately, there are people like that. And [Republican opponent Donald Trump] has lifted them up." Even worse, she added, "Now, some of these folks—they are irredeemable."

So much for "the opportunity to leave the dark, angry politics of the past behind us." Again, when exactly was this era of "civility" when Democrats did *not* call a Republican president "racist" or "fascist" or, in the case of President George W. Bush, a warmonger who "lied us into war with Iraq?" Maybe Biden's press secretary can circle back.

The then *New York Times* executive editor, Dean Baquet, hired a Republican, a Trump-hating one mind you, as a regular columnist. Bret Stephens's maiden column concerned his skepticism about climate change alarmism—not about climate change itself, but the alarmism of its proponents. It was a balance that suggested maybe, just maybe, the world might not end in twelve years because of global warming.

This eminently reasonable column angered *New York Times* subscribers. Many denounced Stephens's hiring and canceled their subscriptions.

Later, at a conference, Baquet was asked about this episode.

"One of the arguments people have," he was asked, "is that, look, that there are plenty of places to get news from climate skeptics, if you want to call them that. And they can get it anywhere they want. So, if the *New York Times* is going to stand for something, and embrace the progressive—"

Before the questioner finished, Baquet said: "I would argue...the history of the *New York Times,* that whole section was not created just to have columnists and writers who agreed with the *New York Times.* It was created after the fall of the *Herald Tribune*, and the original publisher of the *New York Times* wanted some of the conservative columnists who worked for the *Herald Tribune*. So it was created as a forum for different voices. I don't understand how one can actually have an intellectual discourse in this country if you cannot have the opportunity to read thoughtful people with whom you disagree. We're at a moment in the country right now which I think, you know, the left should do some soul-searching, too. We don't wanna hear anything—well, not me because I'm a journalist—but the left, as a rule, does not want to hear thoughtful disagreement."

I list all of these instances because in almost all cases, major news outlets go along with whatever narrative Democrats want to push about their opponents.

During my campaign, the most outrageous smears came from black *Los Angeles Times* columnist Erica D. Smith, who writes about "diversity" for the paper.

Smith wrote a number of columns about me throughout the election, but the one that stands out is from August 20, headlined, "Larry Elder is the Black face of white supremacy. You've been warned." In it, she called me "smug" about my positions—and wrote that black people should ignore me.

"I won't lie," Smith wrote. "Few things infuriate me more than watching a black person use willful blindness and cherry-picked facts to make overly simplistic arguments that whitewash the complex problems that come along with being black in America."

Further, she accused me of running to get "attention" and that my ideas were bad for black people.

"Elder opposes every single public policy idea that's supported by black people to help black people," she wrote, adding, "He keeps trotting out statistics that purport to show that black people are particularly prone to murdering one another."

She concluded: "Black people know better than anyone how dangerous Elder is. He is the O.G. troll that no one was supposed to feed. But here we are."

Like other successful black conservatives, I'd been attacked many times by other blacks as a sell-out, Uncle Tom, and a racial traitor for advocating self-reliance and defending the goodness of America. But this one takes the cake.

If Elder is "known for…demonizing black liberals to entertain white conservatives"—as Smith also said—does this also mean Smith entertains white liberals (the *Los Angeles Times'* primary readership) by demonizing black conservatives?

After the race, I invited Erica Smith on my show. First, she denied receiving the invitation, despite the fact that I made it on Twitter and Facebook, on the air, and by email sent directly to her. She emailed back, "I've said all I need to say about Larry Elder during the campaign and in my columns."

Then there's the *Los Angeles Times'* Latina columnist Jean Guerrero, who also pushed the white supremacy lie in a piece headlined: "If Larry Elder is elected, life will get harder for Black and Latino Californians." In an appearance on CNN, she claimed incredibly: "[Elder has] refused to talk to nonpartisan media outlets and to journalists who are critical of him, has refused to answer difficult questions…But he has been able to reach the minority of voters in California who embrace his white supremacist worldview."

Actually, Elder (that's me) gave two contentious "interviews" with hostile editorial board members of the *Los Angeles Times* and the *Sacramento Bee,* both of which supported Newsom's election and opposed his recall. One can watch these interviews on YouTube.

Guerrero—not a *Los Angeles Times* board member—attempted to participate in that paper's interview, and I refused to allow her to do so.

Poor Guerrero, denied a well-deserved opportunity to ask an innocent question after accusing me of being a "white supremacist." And yet it was her fellow columnist, Erica Smith, who had refused to talk to me by declining several invitations to appear on my radio show and defend her "white supremacist" slur.

Finally, at the start of my interview with the *Los Angeles Times,* I asked whether they concurred with their columnist's assertion that I'm "the black face of white supremacy." They ducked the question, refusing to condemn the comment or its author.

All of this demonstrates that for Democrats and their lackeys in the media, there is only one way to be black—and that is from the left-wing.

Chapter 8

THE TRUTH ABOUT RACE IN AMERICA

THE COVER OF THE FEBRUARY 18, 2022, edition of *Newsweek* featured some black conservatives, including Winsome Sears, John James, Herschel Walker, Vernon Jones, Candace Owens, and me. All the others were painted standing while I was seated, looking into the distance in deep thought.

The topline read: "The rise of Black Conservatives could be pivotal in the 2022 elections—and beyond."[55] We were all pictured with serious looks except for Herschel, who is always smiling, and Sears, the recently elected lieutenant governor of Virginia whom I consider to be a remarkable breath of fresh air for our party.

Inside, the article by Steve Friess had another title: "GOP Bets on Black Conservatives as Key to Victory: 'We Change or We Die.'"

---

55 Steve Friess, "GOP Bets on Black Conservatives as Key to Victory: 'We Change or We Die,'" *Newsweek*, February 9, 2022, https://www.newsweek.com/2022/02/18/gop-bets-black-conservatives-key-victory-we-change-we-die.

In the online version, an upbeat video started off with Sears, noting that she was the first black woman elected to statewide office in Virginia and received 17 percent of the black vote, more than any other GOP statewide candidate. Likewise, John James, running for a House seat in suburban Detroit, became Michigan's first elected black Republican member of Congress. *Newsweek* noted the results of my unsuccessful California recall campaign but added, "However, he gained the support of black, Asian, and Latino communities that typically lean Democratic. (Thank you, *Newsweek*!) Obviously, this was a big sea change for the GOP, across the country.

First-term House member Byron Donalds of Florida explained the explosion of black Republican candidates this way: "It's not just about black conservatives rising and seeing their success. There's a lot of black people witnessing how diabolical the Democrats are when it comes to trying to maintain their monopoly on black folks. They're sick of it, they're deciding to make a change, and they're deciding to run for office."

Johns Hopkins political science professor Leah Wright Rigueur, author of the 2016 book *The Loneliness of the Black Republican*, explained the necessary mechanics: "[It's] not about winning one hundred percent of the black folks, it's not even about winning fifty percent. It is about winning just enough to push them over the edge and make the difference."

Republican National Committee spokesman Paris Dennard, the first black person to hold that position in the RNC, pointed to the 2021 Virginia election that put Winsome Sears in office and noted that black Democrats lost to white Republicans in regions with sizable black constituencies.

Noting that Donald Trump's share of the black vote was 12 percent, the highest percentage for a GOP presidential nominee since Ronald Reagan took 14 percent in 1980, Dennard told the *Newsweek* journalist that the current rise of black GOP candidates "started with President Trump and how vocal he was about the Black Voices for Trump movement being fully funded and staffed."

I pointed out that Donald Trump, to a greater degree than any Republican presidential candidate I've seen, went to the inner city and tried to get black votes. "The message is this: Don't act as if black people cannot be convinced. They can be. Don't condescend. Tell the truth. Talk about the issues, talk about how these issues benefit you."

The article stated that "Black Americans have been the country's most loyal voting bloc for either party, with more than 95 percent of Black voters registering Democratic or voting in Democratic primaries," but it also quoted Hopkins professor Leah Rigueur as saying, "Democrats have historically supported civil rights."

Really?

I guess she must have forgotten about Southern Democrat segregationist governors like George Wallace and Lester Maddox back in the 1960s and 1970s and Al Gore's father, Albert Arnold Gore Sr.—the Democratic senator from Tennessee who not only voted against the Civil Rights Act of 1964 but filibustered against it—or the fact that, as a percentage of the party, more Republicans voted for the Civil Rights Act of 1964 than did Democrats.

Those in the media "forget" about the Democratic party's history of racism all the time. I watched former Clinton staffer and ABC host George Stephanopoulos interview the now attorney general of Minnesota, Keith Ellison, at the Democratic Convention in 2016. At the time, Ellison, a Democratic congressman, was the cochair of the Congressional Progressive Caucus.

Stephanopoulos said to Ellison: "You're a supporter of Bernie Sanders. What should happen?"

Ellison replied: "Well, I'm with Bernie on this. I mean, we're focused on getting rid of Donald Trump, making sure he is not the president of the United States. I agree with Bernie. I'm disappointed to read about it, but at the same time, you know, we do have the worst Republican nominee since George Wallace. We have somebody who is so dangerous, in a number of ways, not the least of which is his attacks on the press, in his pulling press credentials. The First Amendment says freedom of the press. He attacks the press regularly."

Unfortunately for Ellison—and for Stephanopoulos, who failed to correct him—on the panel sat Oklahoma Republican Tom Cole, who said: "First, I want to correct my friend. George Wallace was a proud Democrat and ran for the Democratic nomination. He was on that stage down there."

"And thank god he got rejected and lost!" Ellison said.

Cole replied, "Well, that's fine, but let's be clear on the record whose party he belonged to."[56]

As recently as 1956, nearly 39 percent of blacks voted Republican in that year's presidential election. After the Civil

56 This Week Transcript: "Live from Philadelphia Democratic National Convention," ABC News, July 24, 2016, https://abcnews.go.com/ThisWeek/week-transcript-live-philadelphia-democratic-national-convention/story?id=40825144.

War, Abe Lincoln's Republican Party easily carried the black vote—where blacks were allowed to vote. Unwelcome in the Democratic Party, most blacks voted Republican and continued to do so through the early part of the twentieth century. It wasn't until 1948, when 77 percent of the black vote went to Harry Truman who had desegregated the military, that a majority of blacks identified themselves as Democrats.

Yet, as a percentage of the party, more Republicans voted for the passage of the Civil Rights Act of 1964 than did Democrats. For his key role in breaking the Democrats' filibuster and getting the act to pass the stalled Senate, Republican senator Everett Dirksen, a conservative from Illinois, landed on the cover of *Time* magazine. President Lyndon Johnson called Dirksen "the hero of the nation." The *Chicago Defender*, then the country's largest black daily newspaper, applauded Dirksen's "generalship" for helping to push through the bill.

Five decades of lies helped Democrats create the monolithic black vote. And now that they're losing their hold on blacks, they've resorted to other, more desperate games.

Older black voters sometimes explain they're opposed to Republicans because of the "racist" Southern strategy. But Richard Nixon speechwriter Pat Buchanan, credited with inventing the "Southern strategy," considered the Democratic Party the party of the racists. Buchanan said: "We would build our Republican Party on a foundation of states' rights, human rights, small government and a strong national defense, and leave it to the 'party of [Georgia Democratic governor Lester] Maddox, [1966 Democratic challenger against Spiro Agnew for Maryland governor George] Mahoney and [Alabama Democratic governor George] Wallace to squeeze the last ounces of political juice out of the rotting fruit of racial injustice.'"

But before that, another pivotal event occurred that helped the GOP-as-racist meme. In 1960, during the presidential campaign, Martin Luther King Jr. was arrested following a sit-in at a segregated lunch counter in Atlanta. Hundreds of other protestors were released, but King was jailed on a trumped-up probation violation charge for failing to have a Georgia driver's license.

King's aides reached out to then vice president and Republican presidential candidate, Richard Nixon. They also reached out to the Democratic nominee, John F. Kennedy. Bobby Kennedy called the Atlanta judge handling the case. Shortly after that call, the judge released King. According to civil rights activist Harry Belafonte, Nixon had done "nothing." But is that true?

Nixon, it turns out, had a much closer relationship with King than did Kennedy. In the Nixon Presidential Library in Yorba Linda, California, records show considerable handwritten notes and correspondence between Nixon and King. This includes a 1957 letter from King acknowledging their previous meetings, which thanked Nixon for his "assiduous labor and dauntless courage in seeking to make the Civil Rights Bill a reality" and praised him for his "devotion to the highest mandates of the moral law."

But in 1960, on the eve of the election, Nixon was in a tough spot. His public silence might be misconstrued as acceptance of King's arrest. On the other hand, as a candidate for his boss's job, Nixon worried about the political costs of appearing ungrateful if he chastised President Eisenhower for not taking stronger action. Eisenhower, for his part, was content to let the Justice Department handle the matter.

According to historian and presidential biographer Stephen Ambrose, while Nixon made no public comments, he telephoned Attorney General William Rogers to find out if King's constitutional rights were being infringed, thus opening the door for federal involvement. Nixon, a lawyer, was concerned about the ethics of calling a judge to get him to release someone.

Nixon, writes Ambrose, told his press secretary: "I think Dr. King is getting a bum rap. But despite my strong feelings in this respect, it would be completely improper for me or any other lawyer to call the judge. And Robert Kennedy should have known better than to do so." That Bobby Kennedy, also a lawyer, and later US Attorney General in his brother's administration, nevertheless made a phone call to the judge did not alter the issue of whether it was appropriate. In retrospect, an easy call, but not at the time.

Two million pamphlets were distributed in black churches titled, "No Comment—Nixon Versus a Candidate with a Heart, Senator Kennedy." Never mind that in 1956 Nixon revealed he was an honorary member of the NAACP. Or that he pushed for passage of the '57 civil rights bill in the Senate. Or that *Time* magazine wrote that Nixon's support for civil rights incurred the wrath of one of his segregationist opponents, Senator Richard Russell, D-Georgia, who sarcastically called him the NAACP's "most distinguished member."

But the GOP-is-racist meme can be heard nightly on MSNBC and in political science and history classes all over the country. Keeping blacks ignorant of history remains crucial to this caricature of the Republican Party—and to the monolithic Democratic black vote. Democratic Party indoctrination runs deep and erases memory.

A quote from Youngkin's running mate Winsome Sears, a grandmother and ex-Marine, summed up the perfect attitude for the GOP going forward in getting the black vote: "The Democrats can keep taking people for granted at their peril. But I don't even want all black people to become Republicans. I just don't want you to know how I will vote based on my skin color. If you already think you know how I will vote, then I have no political power. I want you to come and ask us for our vote."

Sears's feelings are echoed in a *Newsweek* opinion article by Kitara Johnson entitled "We Need More Black Voices—But Not Only Ones That Agree With Each Other."[57] A national diversity and inclusion trainer and chief human resource officer, Johnson wrote about "another form of suppression we face: the silencing of black voices that are different and the constant attempts to shame dissenters into compliance." She pointed out that "People like Dave Chapelle or Senator Tim Scott or Morgan Freeman or Condoleezza Rice are smeared as sellouts who betrayed their race for refusing to say what others want them to. And this behavior is supported by the liberal establishment across the board."

Soul sister!

Even bleeding-heart liberals such as Morgan Freeman recognize this in their better moments. Freeman once said to

57 Kitara Johnson, "We Need More Black Voices—But Not Only Ones that Agree with Each Other," *Newsweek*, February 14, 2022, https://www.newsweek.com/we-need-more-black-voices-not-only-ones-that-agree-each-other-opinion-1679092.

Mike Wallace on *60 Minutes* that we could better race relations by not obsessing over it:

WALLACE: "Black History Month, you fin..."

FREEMAN: "Ridiculous."

WALLACE: "Why?"

FREEMAN: "You're going to relegate my history to a month?"

WALLACE: "Come on."

FREEMAN: "What do you do with yours? Which month is White History Month? Come on, tell me."

WALLACE: "I'm Jewish."

FREEMAN: "OK. Which month is Jewish History Month?"

WALLACE: "There isn't one."

FREEMAN: "Why not? Do you want one?"

WALLACE: "No, no."

FREEMAN: "I don't either. I don't want a Black History Month. Black history is American history."

WALLACE: "How are we going to get rid of racism until...?"

> **FREEMAN:** "Stop talking about it. I'm going to stop calling you a white man. And I'm going to ask you to stop calling me a black man. I know you as Mike Wallace. You know me as Morgan Freeman. You're not going to say, 'I know this white guy named Mike Wallace.' Hear what I'm saying?"[58]

I agree entirely. Almost sixty years ago, Martin Luther King Jr. said: "I have a dream that my four little children will one day live in a nation where they will not be judged by the color of their skin but by the content of their character."

Well, I have my own dream. I want all politicians judged by the quality of the policies they put into practice, not by empty emotional rhetoric. When we get to that point in California and our country, *Newsweek* might not have a cover featuring people based on the color of their skin. Instead, they will feature people lauded for what they have done to give us all a much better society.

But as things stand right now, it is in Democrats' interest to prevent my dream from ever becoming reality. And yet, even though it benefits Republicans (not to mention everyone else) that people be judged on their merits rather than their skin color, few Republicans are calling for this. Why? They're afraid of getting called *racist*. Their silence is deafening.

All of these problems were supposed to be solved with the election of Barack Obama. I was in Boston in 2004 when he gave the endorsement speech for John Kerry and brought

---

58 The Rubin Report, "Morgan Freeman Silences '60 Minutes' Host By Insulting Black History Month," YouTube, February 3, 2022, https://www.youtube.com/watch?v=RosCZkH5uTI.

down the house. I turned to my producer and said, "This man is going to run for president someday and there's a good chance he's going to get elected." And, of course, I was proven right. I didn't vote for him because I don't vote for more regulation, tax-and-spend Democrats. But back then, I respected how he spoke about racial tension.

The first time Obama gave a major interview was on *60 Minutes.* He was not yet the front runner, but he was gaining on Hillary, otherwise CBS wouldn't put him on. Correspondent Steve Croft said, "Senator, if you don't get the nomination, will it be because of race?" Obama said, "No, if I don't win, it will be because I have not articulated a vision that the American people can embrace."[59] And I said, hallelujah, at least this guy will bury the knife into the notion that America is systemically racist. And just because you're black, doesn't mean you can't become president.

At a 2007 speech at Brown Chapel A.M.E. Church, presidential candidate Obama talked about the black struggle, how much had been achieved, and that which remained: "The previous generation, the Moses generation, pointed the way. They took us 90% of the way there. But we still got that 10% in order to cross over to the other side."[60]

This is the Obama the American people assumed they had hired in November 2008. Hopeful, positive, a liberal Democrat

59 "Obama 2007: Launching His Candidacy," CBS 60 Minutes, https://www.cbsnews.com/news/obama-2007-launching-his-candidacy/.

60 Barack Obama, Remarks at the Selma Voting Rights March Commemoration in Selma, Alabama, The American Presidency Project, March 4, 2007, https://www.presidency.ucsb.edu/documents/remarks-the-selma-voting-rights-march-commemoration-selma-alabama.

to be sure, but a black man who could serve, at the very least, as a racial reconciler, keenly aware of how far America has come.

When he entered the Oval Office in the third week of January 2009, his approval rating approached 70 percent. A January 2009 ABC News poll found that 58 percent thought race relations would improve under Obama. But by October 2016, one month before the presidential election, a CNN/ORC poll found 54 percent thought race relations *worsened* under Obama, including 40 percent of blacks and 57 percent of whites.

But every time Obama had a chance to show us that he was that guy I hoped for, he picked up the race card instead. Early in Obama's first term, an incident in the elite liberal haven of Cambridge, Massachusetts, gave him a golden opportunity to defuse the lie that the police engage in "systemic racism" against blacks. The Cambridge police briefly arrested Harvard professor Henry Louis Gates, a famous black writer and a personal friend of Obama, in his own home. Gates, returning from a trip, couldn't open his front door and reportedly asked his driver to help. A neighbor, observing two people she did not recognize trying to force open the front door of Gates's home, called 911. The cops arrived and politely asked Gates to exit the home and show his ID so the police could determine ownership. Instead, Gates mouthed off and was briefly arrested.

Obama ill-advisedly weighed in. He said, "The Cambridge police acted stupidly."[61] But the Cambridge Police Superior Officers Association and the Cambridge police commissioner

61 Ben Smith, "Obama: Cambridge Police Acted 'Stupidly,'" *POLITICO*, July 22, 2009, https://www.politico.com/blogs/ben-smith/2009/07/obama-cambridge-police-acted-stupidly.

insisted the officer simply followed protocol as any homeowner would want them to do. Obama's statement infuriated officers all across the country and he later had to walk back his comments, even inviting the offending officer to the White House for a beer with the president of the United States. But the incident set up a template for the Obama administration: Cops systemically engage in antiblack racial profiling.

Suppose Obama had not insultingly denounced the Cambridge police. Suppose, instead, Obama had said: "I've just spoken to my friend, Professor Gates. I reminded him that he is a role model and that his behavior with the Cambridge police officer, who was merely doing his job, was unacceptable. We need to understand as Americans that officers typically have a difficult job. Yes, there are some bad cops, but for the most part, they're trying to do their best. And contrary to popular perception, the police, in recent years, have killed more unarmed whites than blacks. It is a lie, not supported by the evidence, that cops are killing blacks just because they're black. This is not Jim Crow America. It is our job as civilians to be respectful, polite and by all means, comply. Comply; you won't die."

Suppose Obama encouraged blacks to comply with the police and that if one feels mistreated, to get a name or badge number and sort it out later. Eric Garner died after an encounter where New York City cops arrested him for selling cigarettes. Had he not resisted, he likely would be alive today. Jacob Blake was shot several times by the Kenosha, Wisconsin police when they suspected him of reaching for a knife. Had Blake complied, he would not be in a wheelchair today. Would that have encouraged black suspects like George Floyd to respond differently to an encounter with the police?

Obama knows the statistics. He knows the studies. He knows there is no evidence of antiblack "systemic racism" on the part of the police. But the political Obama knows that black anger and resentment translate into black votes. How many routine police encounters with blacks escalate into something far more serious because young blacks believe the "systemic racism" lie pushed by Black Lives Matter, an activist organization based on the false narrative of police "systemic racism" against blacks, and their sympathizers?

Obama, as president, peddled—with little evidence—an ever-growing list of racial grievances. The list included the Cambridge police incident; his comments that racism is "still part of our DNA" and "if I had a son, he'd look like Trayvon" holding Ferguson up as a microcosm of racial strife in America; inviting race-hustling incendiary Reverend Al Sharpton to the White House over seventy times; and embracing the Black Lives Matter movement.

Obama rarely missed an opportunity not to be the conciliator Americans thought him to be. He knows that racism has never been a less significant factor as an obstacle to American success. His very election and reelection stand as a testament to that truth.

Obama won the presidency based on a lie. He entered the presidency as an articulate, even-tempered, racial unifier and left as an articulate, even-tempered, racial incendiary. Today, he plays the race card from his $12 million estate on Martha's Vineyard.

Similarly, Obama's Harvard Law–educated attorney general Eric Holder made race relations worse. When he entered office, he said that when it comes to matters of race, "America has been a nation of cowards."[62] Holder gave three examples of what he called "pernicious racism:" voter ID laws; longer prison sentences for black criminals who commit the same crime as whites; and higher rates of expulsion for black students from schools compared to the expulsion rates of other racial groups.

Holder is wrong, wrong, wrong. Let's examine his charges.

Holder considers voter ID laws as racist, or more precisely, that those who want them do so to suppress minority voter turnout. Holder said: "In too many jurisdictions, new types of restrictions are justified as attempts to curb an epidemic of voter fraud that—in reality—has never been shown to exist. Rather than addressing a supposedly widespread problem, these policies disproportionately disenfranchise African Americans, Hispanics, other communities of color, and vulnerable populations such as the elderly. But interfering with or depriving a person of the right to vote should never be a political aim. It is a moral failing."

One problem with Holder's argument is that most white, Hispanic and black voters support voter photo ID. A 2016 Gallup poll found broad support for photo voter ID—95 percent of Republicans, 83 percent of Independents, 63 percent of Democrats, and 77 percent of nonwhites.

62 Associated Press Staff, "AG Eric Holder: Subtle, Institutionalized Racism More Pernicious than Bigoted Outbursts," FOX NEWS, January 8, 2015, https://www.foxnews.com/us/ag-eric-holder-subtle-institutionalized-racism-more-pernicious-than-bigoted-outbursts.

As far as the supposedly onerous nature of the law, in 2008, the Supreme Court ruled six to three that such laws do not impose any undue burden on voters. Justice John Paul Stevens, arguably the court's most liberal member, wrote the majority opinion in this case about Indiana voter ID. Stevens wrote, "There is no question about the legitimacy or importance of the State's interest in counting only the votes of eligible voters. Moreover, the interest in orderly administration and accurate recordkeeping provides a sufficient justification for carefully identifying all voters participating in the election process. While the most effective method of preventing election fraud may well be debatable, the propriety of doing so is perfectly clear."

Georgia lawmakers, to increase voter integrity, passed a series of changes that critics decried as anti-black "voter suppression." What happened? In its most recent election, the percentage of eligible blacks who voted exceeded the percentage of eligible whites who voted, a pattern that has become the case in presidential elections, as well. The "suppress the vote" narrative is a con.

Then MSNBC host Chris Matthews, a former Democratic Hill staffer, told Holder's successor, former attorney general Loretta Lynch, that Republicans push voter ID laws to "screw the African-American voter." Lynch responded: "Yes, yes—and it's nothing new...This is a historical issue. It's a current issue. And it's only history because it happened to somebody else, not because it could never happen again. That's what's happening now."

Then vice president Joe Biden called Trump's assertion that millions of people voted illegally in the 2016 election a "flat lie." But Biden did not stop there. The Republican support for voter ID, he said, was all about suppressing minority votes. "It's what these guys are all about, man. Republicans don't want working-class people voting. They don't want black folks voting." Senator Elizabeth Warren, D-Massachusetts, denounced "racist voter ID laws and voter-suppression tactics [that] sprout like weeds all across the country." In 2017 CNN's April Ryan asked then White House press secretary Sarah Sanders: "So, Sarah, since you keep saying that the president is very concerned about the election process...you did not mention voter suppression in that. Voter suppression has been an issue for decades and particularly in these last few elections." Despite these alleged racist roadblocks to the ballot box, in 2008 blacks voted at a higher percentage than whites.

The fact that voter ID is legal and popular does not, of course, affect the view held by many on the left that it "suppresses" the minority vote. The George Soros–supported website *ThinkProgress* ran a story last year with this menacing headline: "New study confirms that voter ID laws are very racist."

Citing research by three professors from UC San Diego, Michigan State, and Bucknell University, the article says: "turnout among Hispanic voters is '7.1 percentage points lower in general elections and 5.3 points lower in primaries' in states with strict voter ID laws. The laws also reduce turnout among African-American and Asian-American voters. White turnout, according to their study, is 'largely unaffected.'"[63]

63 Ian Millhiser, "New Study Confirms that Voter ID Laws Are Very Racist," Think Progress, February 17, 2017, https://archive.thinkprogress.org/new-study-confirms-that-voter-id-laws-are-very-racist-c338792c3f04/.

Case closed? Not exactly.

A follow-up study by researchers from Yale, Stanford, and the University of Pennsylvania found no evidence that voter ID laws have a statistically significant impact on voter turnout. This study examined the methodology and conclusions of the previous study. Its researchers wrote: "Widespread concern that voter identification laws suppress turnout among racial and ethnic minorities has made empirical evaluations of these laws crucial. But problems with administrative records and survey data impede such evaluations...We show that the results of the paper are a product of data inaccuracies [and] the presented evidence does not support the stated conclusion... When errors are corrected, one can recover positive, negative or null estimates of the effect of voter ID laws on turnout, precluding firm conclusions."[64]

In other words, the data do not support the notion that blacks are too dumb, too lazy, or incapable of obtaining the necessary identification to vote.

Let's turn to Holder's assertion that different rates of expulsion from school is a sign of "pernicious" racism.

Holder correctly noted that black students, when compared to their percentage in the school's population, are suspended at disproportionately higher rates. To Holder, this spells racism: "Codified segregation of public schools has been barred since Brown. But in too many of our school districts, significant divisions persist and segregation has reoc-

64 Justin Hersh, Marc Meredith, Jonathan Mummolo, and Clayton Nall, "Obstacles to Estimating Voter ID Laws' Effect on Turnout," The University of Chicago Press Journals, Volume 80, Number 3, https://www.journals.uchicago.edu/doi/abs/10.1086/696618?af=R&.

curred—including zero-tolerance school discipline practices that, while well intentioned and aimed at promoting school safety, affect black males at a rate three times higher than their white peers."

The reverend Jesse Jackson, too, complains about allegedly racist educators who suspend black kids more frequently than they do white ones. Teachers, especially those who work in the inner city, are overwhelmingly left-wing, voted for Obama twice and believe in "progressive" liberal values and social justice. Yet they stand accused of racism or, in the case of black teachers, self-hatred.

In 1999, Jackson filed suit against the Decatur, Illinois, school board over allegations of racism. Seven black high school students were expelled for inciting a brawl at a high school football game. Enter Jackson. "This isn't about black and white," he insisted, "but wrong and right."

Jackson demanded the immediate reenrollment of the students, arguing that the punishment did not fit the crime. Then, oops, a video of the fight surfaced, and Jackson's initial description of a "simple fistfight" did not bear up.

It looked ugly.

Many more people could have been hurt. It turned out the seven students, collectively, had previously missed over three hundred days in their high school careers. Further, the school board pointed to previous behavioral problems on the part of some of the students. The students had gang ties, and one was arrested two more times *following* his suspension. Still, the school board agreed under pressure to cut the suspensions to one year. The governor of Illinois agreed to change policy and allow the students to enroll in an alternative school and receive credit—all so that the seniors involved could still graduate "on time."

Unappeased, Jackson forced authorities to arrest him when he showed up, students by his side, and to demand their immediate re-enrollment. "The schools are 48 percent black and brown," said Jackson, "the teachers and the school board are 90 percent white. This is what happens when you have these culture gaps and stereotypes, and unfounded fears."

Jackson's Rainbow/PUSH Coalition sued the predominantly white Decatur school district, claiming they disproportionately expelled black students, who were 48 percent of the student body but accounted for 82 percent of expulsions.

But Jackson had a big problem in proving his case. Data showed that black kids were disproportionately expelled even in liberal cities like Oakland and San Francisco. The seven-member board of education in San Francisco—ground zero for "compassionate liberalism"—contained one Latino, two Asians, and one black. Blacks were then 16 percent of the student population but 52 percent of the suspensions and expulsions. Similarly, the ten-member Oakland school board—which once announced an ill-conceived, much-criticized Ebonics program to enable teachers to "relate" to their disadvantaged students—included four blacks, two Latinos and two Asians. Yet blacks comprised 52 percent of the students and 73 percent of the suspensions and expulsions.

"Pernicious" racism?

Holder's third example of "pernicious racism," that black criminals receive longer sentences for the same crime as whites because of racism, also falls apart upon examination.

Holder said, "In our criminal justice system, systemic and unwarranted racial disparities remain disturbingly common." Citing the US Sentencing Commission, he said black men are sentenced to prison terms 20 percent longer than are whites who commit similar crimes. "Disparate outcomes," Holder said, "are not only shameful and unacceptable, they impede our ability to see that justice is done...A criminal justice system that treats groups of people differently—and punishes them unequally—has a much more negative impact than misguided words that we can reject out of hand."

But Holder misrepresents the commission's conclusion.

True, they found that black criminal male defendants receive sentences 19.5 percent longer than do white males who commit similar crimes. But, contrary to what the attorney general implied, the sentencing commission never used the term "racism" to explain the gap. The commission said, "[Judges] make sentencing decisions based on many *legitimate* [emphasis added] considerations that are not or cannot be measured."

Twenty-eight years ago, in 1994, the Justice Department surveyed felony cases in the country's seventy five largest urban areas. Is there institutional racism in arresting, trying, and sentencing black criminal defendants? The survey actually found *lower* felony prosecution rates for blacks than whites, and that blacks were less likely to be found guilty at trial. Once convicted, blacks were likely to receive longer sentences than whites, but this disparity was due to differences in the severity of the crime, their prior criminal records, or other legal variables.

Polls rate Barack Obama as one of the most admired people in America, particularly among black Americans. Out of office, he maintains respect, power, stature, and influence. As president, he *could* have saved lives by putting truth over politics. He chose not to.

Obama recently gave a speech in which he attacked the critics of "identity politics." At the June Copenhagen Democracy Summit, Obama said: "I have little sympathy for reactionaries who cynically condemn identity politics or cancel culture when really all they're doing is trying to preserve existing privilege or excuse entrenched injustice, or bigotry. I mean, the original identity politics is racism and sexism and homophobia. That's nothing if not identity politics, and it's done a lot more harm than some tweet from an aggrieved liberal."

"Reactionaries"?

Yes, that would be the same Obama who burst on the national scene by giving a rafter-ringing keynote speech at the Boston 2004 DNC convention where he *denounced* identity politics.

Then Illinois state senator Obama said: "There are those who are preparing to divide us, the spin masters and negative ad peddlers who embrace the politics of anything goes. Well, I say to them tonight, there's not a liberal America and a conservative America—there's the United States of America. There's not a black America and white America and Latino America and Asian America; there's the United States of America. The pundits like to slice-and-dice our country into red states and blue states; red states for Republicans, blue states for Democrats. But I've got news for them, too...We are one people, all of us pledging allegiance to the stars and stripes, all of us defending the United States of America."[65]

Today's Obama would call *that* Obama a "reactionary," making excuses for inequality, exclusion, and bigotry. He might even be called the black face of white supremacy.

Obama should have shot down that narrative when he had the chance. At the very least, with an Elder presidential candidacy, I could change it forever.

---

65 "Barack Obama's Remarks to the Democratic National Convention." *New York Times.* July 27, 2004. https://www.nytimes.com/2004/07/27/politics/campaign/barack-obamas-remarks-to-the-democratic-national.html.

Chapter 9

HOW WE CAN HELP BLACK FAMILIES SUCCEED

HERE IS THE REAL PROBLEM. Racism is no longer a significant factor in American life. In fact, I would say it's a trivial factor now. And I can demonstrate this very easily.

When I was growing up in South Central Los Angeles, "Paul" was one of my closest friends. We knew each other since the second grade, and his father, who was a bus driver, was never involved in his life. His mother cleaned houses. His father and mother separated when he was in kindergarten. Paul was the first boy I knew who did not live with both mother and father. Today, black kids raised by single moms are the norm, but back then, it was rare. Paul rarely spoke of his father and saw him infrequently.

We lived about five blocks away from each other, and our houses were identical. He came over to my house in third grade and looked around.

"Whoever built your house, built mine," he said. When we went over to his house, he pointed out that nearly everything was the same. We had the same teachers, went to the same schools, same everything.

In grade school and junior high, he and I spent countless hours together. He helped me become a slightly better athlete, and I helped him with math and biology. But when I returned home from college, Paul had become "Muhammad."

Pre-Muhammad, Paul starred on the high school basketball, baseball, and football teams. As the basketball team's starting point guard, he was a prolific scorer and a tenacious defender, a combination college recruiters drool over. Big basketball power schools—UCLA, Notre Dame, Marquette, and others—scouted him. Paul talked incessantly about the destiny to which he felt entitled—the NBA, the money, and the glamor.

But Paul had a problem: his temper and arrogance.

Paul routinely came to basketball practice late and then practiced halfheartedly. Come game time, however, he performed brilliantly. For this reason, despite being, as his coach described him, a "hot head," Paul was never benched. Once when Paul came to practice late, the coach finally had enough and for the first and only time, scolded him in front of his teammates. During this long-overdue lecture about responsibility and respect for fellow teammates, Paul removed his jersey, balled it up...and threw it at the coach. He still started the next game.

When the college recruiters asked about Paul's rumored "attitude problem," the coach was honest. Paul, he told recruiters, was a "coach killer." This means a player so irresponsible and disruptive that you're better off without him, no matter how gifted. Bye-bye, UCLA. So long, Notre Dame. Farewell, Marquette. Hello to a non-prestigious, non-basketball-powerhouse school.

Paul was angry. He felt robbed. Did he use his disappointment to redouble his efforts to show that he could, in fact, make it? No. He played indifferently and spent most of his time smoking dope in his dorm. I was never sure if the coach finally cut him or whether Paul just left. The story kept changing.

I didn't see Paul for a few years after that. When I did, he told me to stop calling him Paul. "My name," he said, "is Muhammad."

He'd thrown away all of his trophies, awards, and newspaper clippings. All of that "nonsense," he insisted, "is now in the past." He called himself an "activist" on a mission to right America's racial wrongs. He'd converted to Islam and stopped eating pork. Putting down dope and women, however, was a much more difficult assignment.

Christianity, he informed me, was a "slave religion." I told him that Arab slavers took more blacks from Africa than did European traders—and that the Arab slave trade in Africa continued long after the Europeans stopped. He said I'd been "misled by the 'White Man's' history books." Never mind that literally every historian worldwide agrees on these facts.

He proceeded to tell me about how the "White Man" oppresses black people and works to "hold us back." No matter how hard you try, Paul said, you're "still black in America," an insurmountable impediment. He went on about "slave-owning" Founding Fathers, Jim Crow, and "racial oppression."

I couldn't take it anymore.

"My turn," I said. "You're talking to someone who's known you since second grade. I know what you went through, your experiences. We grew up in the same neighborhood, attended the same schools, and had the same teachers. Whatever the 'White Man' did to you, he did to me. Why am I achieving?

"Kids hated your arrogance. You didn't just beat your opponent, you taunted and ridiculed him while doing it. Remember in elementary school, when the kids voted for the starters for our kickball team? I was voted on. But you were not—even though you were far and away the best player in the class.

"Do you remember what I did?" I asked. "After class, I told the teacher it was unfair that the best athlete in the class did not make the team. Could I give my position to Paul? She should have said 'no,' that Paul needed to learn that his personality could get in his way. Instead, the teacher said, 'OK, I'll give him your slot.' Looking back, this is exactly the kind of special accommodation you got time and time again.

"I know this—'The Man' had nothing to do with your lack of success. I was there. I had a front-row seat. You gave up on yourself. Rather than assume responsibility for your own choices, you found a scapegoat, an excuse, and someone to blame."

And then I really laid it on him.

"Worst of all, you hurt your community. You hurt me. You should be finishing a ten-year career in the NBA. I should have been the lawyer to negotiate your contract. If you want to look at it your way, you impoverished me."

To this day, we don't speak to each other. He's still living in that same house near the one I grew up in, making excuses for his life, and blaming his failure on "racism."

Paul's case was not an isolated incident. A few years ago at a high school reunion, I ran into another old acquaintance, Marcus, who used to be the tallest kid in my class. We chatted a little while until he stopped me.

"I hear your show on the radio and, you know, I know you're doing this to make money for marketing purposes and you don't believe half the things you're saying," he smiled at me.

I didn't smile back.

"Okay," I said. "Name one thing. Name one thing that I'm insincere about."

"Oh, well, you know, some of the things you say."

"Really," I said. "I'm serious. One thing. My memory's not that good. It would be hard for me to lie and remember all the lies I make. Tell me something."

He couldn't come up with anything.

"You know what I think, Marcus?" I said. "I think you think that racism is a major problem in America. I don't. And you don't like that. That's why you can't think of a single example."

I had a similar interaction with another classmate back in high school. This kid, Gilbert, was popular but kind of lazy. He wasn't necessarily a delinquent, but he preferred to wear cool glasses and flirt with girls than apply himself to anything for very long.

Now, at this time, I had quit working for my dad, and I decided to get a job with the county. To do that, I had to go downtown and take a big, three-hour exam along with about four hundred other people. It wasn't exactly difficult: math, reading comprehension, and the like. After you took the test, you had to wait for it to be graded, and if you passed, they would call your name at the end. If your name wasn't called, you had to leave.

Well, who should I run into downtown but Gilbert? He was also there to take the test, but he was certain he would fail. Before we sat down, he looked around and pointed out to me that most of the other test-takers were white.

"Watch out, they're going to get us," he said.

I just looked at him

"What are you talking about?"

"They're going to find out who the black people are. And we're all not going to pass. They're going to fail us."

And sure enough, Gilbert failed, but I passed. On the way out the door, he leaned over to me, looking angry.

"What did I tell you?" he said.

"What did I tell you?" How did that make any sense? We were both black. I passed, because I cared about passing. He didn't, because he thought the system was rigged against him anyway.

Taken together, all three of these cases tell me that the problem is not "racism" imposed on black people by whites but instead a problem where blacks buy into a narrative that they are oppressed. Everywhere I look, I find anger and people inventing new stories about "enduring racism," "systemic racism," and "pervasive racism." They have to keep coming up with a new villain because this narrative is not working anymore.

All of that stuff was true a long time ago, but we settled it in the last fifty years. How does a guy named Barack Hussein Obama get elected president, beat Hillary, then get reelected with a lousy economic recovery if America is "systemically racist"? That phrase is just a code word—an excuse for different kinds of bitching, whining, and characterizing black people as victims. And it's why white people load themselves down with guilt about cultural appropriation and microaggressions—this is all nonsensical stuff that people on the left come up with in order to justify supporting continued anger by people who have not heard the truth.

And the truth is very simple. The truth is you have to work hard. You have to invest in yourself. You have to accept deferred gratification. You have to get an education. You have to learn a skill. That's why people are begging to get into this country. Not because it's "systemically racist," but because it's a land of opportunity.

But for success to come more readily, there are a couple of baseline things that every child needs. The first is the family, where both the mother and the father are in the home. In my childhood neighborhood now, 70 percent of black kids do not have a father married to the mother in the home. When I was a kid in the late fifties and early sixties that was rare. Now it is rare to have a mother and father in the house if you are a black kid living in the inner city. It is the genesis of all the social problems: crime, dropouts, and people that are not competitive in our economy.

This should not be a controversial point, but it is.

When I was on the campaign trail, I had a Zoom call with several black pastors. I said the number one problem facing

America is not systemic racism, it's the large number of black kids who enter the world without a father married to the mother. I listed off the unintended negative consequences. They went nuts. They insisted that the top problem was systemic racism and I was downplaying it.

"You people are supposed to be leaders," I said. "You are principle setters, and you're attacking me for recognizing the major problem in the black community. This is why we're in the distress that we're in right now."

I wouldn't back off, and I could see that they really believed I was wrong. One of them even told me that he was going to vote for me until I brought it up. I was saddened. The church was what helped black people survive through slavery and segregation. And now these pastors basically preach that a father is not necessary or don't even raise the issue. If they got that pissed off when I pointed it out, I can only imagine what they're saying in their churches on Sunday.

A 2021 article in *Newsweek* argued that my candidacy in the recall election was "the moment of truth for the Christian Left preaching reparations and support of the disadvantaged to support a candidate like Elder."[66] It added: "After all, regardless of Governor Newsom's record leading the state of California, as a multi-millionaire intertwined by blood, marriage, and money to previous California Democrats and political families including the Browns, the Pelosis, and the Gettys, there's no debating he's the epitome of white privilege."

---

66 Carly Mayberry, "A Black Man from South Central, Why Doesn't the Christian Left Back Larry Elder?" *Newsweek*, August 11, 2021, https://www.newsweek.com/black-man-south-central-why-doesnt-christian-left-back-larry-elder-1618422.

What is the Christian Left afraid of? Is it my pro-life position? Before Reverend Jesse Jackson decided to run for president in 1984, he was pro-life, but he realized it was an untenable position for someone running as a Democrat. Was Jackson, before his conversion, an "abortion extremist"?

I am grateful, however, for the handful of pastors who are doing the crucial work of telling their congregations the truth about the black family. In one of my documentaries, we interviewed a pastor who felt strongly about the problem of fatherless families.

"Please, if you are a single mother, don't tell your kid that he's better off without a father," he said. "Don't tell your kid this is normal. Don't tell the kid that this is God's way because it is not."

During my campaign, he invited me to speak at the church and share this message with some frequency at a church in Fresno. Jim and Cyndi Franklin are senior pastors of the Cornerstone Church in downtown Fresno. They've been there for over twenty-five years. Originally from Oklahoma, they worked in ministry together as youth pastors, evangelists, and pastors for over thirty-five years. The church, with a weekly attendance of over two thousand, has an expressed mandate of "Bringing Our City Back to God." On the Thursday before my Sunday appearance at Cornerstone on August 22, 2021, Pastor Franklin posted a short video to his congregation on the Cornerstone Facebook page.

I told them many things related to the campaign, but most importantly, I talked about the eight-hour talk with my father that turned my life around when I was twenty-five years old. I shared my father's philosophy: "Hard work wins. You get out of life what you put into it. You cannot control the outcome, but you are one hundred percent in control of the effort. And before you complain about what somebody did to you or said to you, go to the nearest mirror, look at it and say, what could I have done to change the outcome? And no matter how good you are, how hard you work, sooner or later, bad things are gonna happen to you. How you deal with those bad things will tell your mother and me if we raised a man."

I discussed liberal lies and gave them facts to counter them, including the fact that, contrary to popular belief, cops kill more unarmed white men than unarmed black men. I talked about the Ferguson Effect, now called the George Floyd Effect. Police are increasingly engaging in passive policing, not proactive policing. Even then Chicago mayor Rahm Emanuel said the police in the city had "gone fetal" due to fear of false allegations of "systemic racism."

I talked about how the anticop message encourages young, often fatherless, black men to refuse to comply with lawful instructions, unnecessarily increasing the chances of a cop shooting or killing a suspect. I turned to the case of Baltimore and Freddie Gray, a black man who died in police custody. Three of the six officers charged were black. Two elected to have their cases tried by a judge who happened to be black. He found them not guilty. The top two leaders of the police department were black. The mayor was black. The city council was all Democrat and majority black. The state attorney who filed the charges against the six officers was black, as were US Attorney General Loretta Lynch and the president of the United States. As black comedian Wanda Sykes said about

Obama, "How you gonna complain about the man, when you ARE the man?"

Racism, I said, has never been a less significant problem in America. I brought up the *Los Angeles Times* calling me the "black face of white supremacy." Don't laugh; "I worked hard for that title." How dare I note that 70 percent of black children enter the world without a father married to the mother and that 50 percent of the homicide victims in this country are black. The number one cause of preventable death for young white men is accidents, like car accidents or drowning. The number one cause of death, preventable or nonpreventable, for young black men is homicide, almost always by another young black man. Systemic racism is not the problem, I said, and critical race theory and reparations are not the answer.

I promised to push true school choice, so the money should follow the child rather than the other way around. The parent could put the child in a private school, a charter school, a religious school, or could use the money for homeschooling. I said I preferred the term "government school" rather than "public school" because it highlights the monopolistic nature of the system and the power relations involved and noted that 80 percent of the kids in government schools are black and brown. The Left prides itself on caring about black and brown kids, but we should judge them by their results, not their empty rhetoric. And the fact is that 75 percent of black boys in third grade in California cannot read at state levels of proficiency, with math scores not much better. Half of all third graders in California government schools cannot read at state levels of proficiency, with test scores near the bottom of all fifty states.

I said that Newsom's largest funder is the teachers' union, the most powerful union in the state. Yet a study found large numbers of government school teachers send their own kids to private schools, as does Newsom himself. In my district in Los Angeles, a government school teacher-parent with a school-aged kid, compared to a private school teacher-parent, is twice as likely to have his or her own child in a private school. This is the equivalent of opening up a restaurant and putting up a sign saying, "Come on in! Eat the food. We sure won't!"

This actually gets into the second most important thing that every child needs: a proper education. The family is the most important, but school is a close second. In fact, I'd said that success in the second most often flows from the first.

But right now, schools don't offer much more than a rubber-stamp validation to people from households where the kids are not receiving encouragement and expectations set at home. They are being treated the way McDonald's treats its customers: "Over 1 billion served." Because that's essentially all that happens. The kid shows up, stands in line, and receives his diploma, just like he gets a burger at a fast-food restaurant. It has no nutritional value, and he can't exchange it for anything of value either. But at least he's successful on paper.

Most people don't even know how bad their education was. Let's say you're one of these kids who actually goes through school and doesn't drop out and doesn't join a gang. You still have no skills, and you can't be competitive with your peers. What happens?

You go to a junior college, and you end up having to take remedial math or English because you didn't get it in high school. You fall behind because you started behind. You are always going to be behind. You can make it up, but it's going to be hard.

I have a friend in Cleveland who was a public school teacher. One time, I went to visit her, and she took me to the top student in the school. I spoke with this young lady. She had horrible grammar and said things like "ain't." I mentioned it to my friend, and she got pissed off at me for being condescending.

"This is the best student?" I said. "You hear what she said and how she spoke? What kind of education are you giving these kids? You have to be grading them all on a curve, so the average person is not particularly literate and so somebody who's a little more literate than nothing comes out number one."

We had a fight, but my position remained the same: "This is outrageous. Where are your standards?"

The lack of standards is part of the reason why I feel so strongly about school choice. And I have personal experience with it. When I was at Crenshaw High School, I was considered a good student. I made A's in every class without much thought at all. Sometime in high school, I had taken all the Spanish that Crenshaw had to offer. But, I wanted to take some more, so I applied to a program called Area Program Enrichment Exchange, which a consortium of high schools belonged to. To take more Spanish, I had to go to a high school called Fairfax, which at the time was all Jewish.

When I walked into class on the first day, I was met with a surprise. Every kid in the class was fluent in Spanish, and not in a halting way. The teacher was strict—no one was allowed to speak in English during class, which was not the case in my high school.

For the first time in my life, I found that I was getting F's. When I came home on the first day, I was crying. I told my mother that I felt that I had been ripped off. I felt the expectations set for me at Crenshaw were too low. I knew that I was as smart as these kids were. If I had the same level of expectation put on me for all the years they had, I would have been better than most of them.

My mother started crying too.

"We should have had you in a better, more competitive school," she said. "But we couldn't afford it. Maybe someday you can grow up and do something about it."

The final exam in the class required me to do a book report. The assignment was to write it in Spanish and then stand up and deliver it in Spanish. My report was on *Don Quixote*. I never worked harder on a project in my life.

When the time came to deliver it, I was the ninth person in the class to stand up. After the first eight reports, the teacher offered a critique: she corrected grammar or pronunciation or whatever else was wrong in the presentation. And she was pretty hard on the kids. But after my report, she, along with the class, was completely silent. She had no criticism. I sat down knowing I had done well.

That experience showed me that I could have realized my potential in all sorts of other things if I had that kind of expectation all my life. But I didn't. Crenshaw was like a lot of other inner-city high schools; it was important to dress well and be cool with women, but there was little emphasis on academics.

The Spanish report made me realize that I was at the wrong school and I should have had a better education.

A lot of other black people who've had to fight their way to success are beneficiaries of school choice. Oddly, though, I've noticed that many of them oppose it just the same. Michelle Obama took advantage of school choice, and Barack Obama did in his way, too. He was living in Indonesia with his mom and his stepfather, and she felt he was getting an insufficient education. So his mother sent him back to live with his white maternal grandparents. And he ended up going to the finest prep school in the state of Hawaii, then Occidental, then Columbia, then Harvard. The man never set foot in a public school himself, and his wife came up through good schools because of school choice, but he opposes it for others. Makes no sense unless you factor in the need of Democrats to cater to the powerful teachers' union, which only seeks to protect its monopoly over our kids.

So what needs to change? Well, first of all, parents need to be able to choose which class they want their kids to be in. But more importantly, schools need to focus more on teaching the basics of reading and writing and less on enhancing "self-esteem." At this point, black kids have higher self-esteem than white kids do and much higher self-esteem than Asian American kids. Black girls have higher self-esteem than white girls and feel better about their bodies than white girls, even though black girls are more likely to be heavier and often more obese than white girls.

So the truth is, black people feel great about themselves. They're not performing well, but they feel wonderful about themselves. When you hear people say, "Well, black people lack self-esteem," rest assured they don't. Look at it this way. The reason there's so much violence in the inner city is that when you disrespect me and you belong to some sort of gang, you've offended me because I have such a high opinion of myself. How dare you not share it? You must have the same high opinion of me as I do.

Another excuse that often gets made for black under-achievement involves the so-called "school to prison pipeline." This makes it sound like cops are standing behind the trees outside the school building waiting to cast nets over young black men and drag them off to prison. After all, it is *hard* to go to jail. I interviewed a black sheriff in South Carolina who told me that with all the diversionary programs that have been started, you really have to work to get in real trouble.

I say it frequently, but the formula for achieving middle-class success is simple: finish high school; don't have a child before the age of twenty; and get married before having the child. Also, get a job and keep the job. Lastly, avoid the criminal justice system. If you do those things, you will not be poor. And if you don't, you will be. Walter Williams showed for years in his research that a black, college-educated couple where both members work has long earned as much as a white, college-educated couple where both work.

So despite what you constantly hear, things really aren't that bad for American blacks. Still, the stereotypes persist. I recall reading an article once about a black female CEO who was in first class on a plane, and the writer said something like, "Little do these men know that among them is a fellow CEO."

When I read that, I thought, *How do you know what these guys are thinking about? They are probably thinking about meeting their quarterly projections.*

Why is it that all of a sudden because a bunch of white men are in first class with a black woman they are automatically assumed to be thinking she doesn't belong? How do you know what they're thinking? And what difference does it make? She's there and they're there. I mean, this whole business about the psychological drama that this black woman must be experiencing sitting in first class with all these white men who don't believe she should be there is nonsense. And this just goes to illustrate the inflamed sensitivity of many black people in America today, seeing personal sleights and anti-black discrimination where they don't necessarily even exist.

You hear a lot of black women say that if you ask them to give their top experiences about racism, they'll tell you they get followed in a department store. There's something to this phenomenon. I had a girlfriend who used to work at the Brown University bookstore. She observed that the people most likely to steal books were black students. And that's why they were the ones who were followed. It wasn't about race. It was about statistical probability.

I asked my mother once if she had the experience of being followed in a department store. She sighed and said, "Larry, I don't know. I'm shopping. If someone wants to follow, whatever. I'm not going to take anything."

I've even experienced it myself. I went to a mall called Tanglewood outside of Ann Arbor with a female fellow black law student. We made our purchase and as we were leaving, a white manager came running out, grabbed the bag I was holding, opened it up because he thought we stole something, and of course we hadn't. And he was stammering and stuttering and apologetic.

My girlfriend was furious. She wanted to file a lawsuit.

"The guy thought that we stole something," I said. "Probably a disproportionately large number of black people come into the store to steal. And so he's on guard. You ought to be angry at the black people stealing. That's undermining our reputation and image instead of being managed and that this guy could do his job."

I mention all this to drive home that whenever someone points out broad, entrenched racism, there's usually a more reasonable explanation for what is happening. Most black people don't see this, so they internalize the idea that "systemic racism" gave them broken families and schools. And most white people are unable to address the real problems, or talk about them honestly, and so they waste time apologizing for racism they did not commit.

When I was a lawyer in the '80s, there was a black golfer in the Masters named Lee Elder. He was all over the news as the first black man in the Masters. So, at that time, whenever someone at the firm introduced me to a client, he would say something along the lines of, "This is my associate, Larry Elder."

And then the client would say, "Nice to meet you, Lee."

And I'd correct him, calmly.

"I'm Larry. Lee Elder is the golfer."

And he'd blush eighteen shades of red.

But I wasn't offended. I'd just tell him to calm down; he just wasn't listening. He was so nervous about meeting a black lawyer that he forgot to remember my name.

Now, Lee Elder is not in the news anymore, so this doesn't happen to me too often. But I have noticed that when white people meet a black person, they are always on their guard. They want to make sure they say the right thing, do the right thing, and are not perceived as insensitive, let alone racist.

Well, that doesn't do much for black people. Their real problems run much deeper than that—and are not determined by skin color. It's time black leadership in this country did something to address them.

This is why I'm running for president.

Chapter 10

THE BATTLE PLAN

SINCE THE RECALL ELECTION, I'VE been watching the growth of California's problems—and their spread all over the country—with increasing dismay. California's massive budget obligations continue to worsen. By the third quarter of 2021, according to the US Bureau of Economic Analysis, California had a 2.7 percent real gross domestic product (GDP) increase. In contrast, the states that Californians were moving to, experienced much higher rates of growth, particularly in states with no state income tax. Tesla relocated to Texas, which had a GDP increase of 3.7 percent. Florida had a GDP increase of 3.8 percent, compared to the average US GDP increase of 2.3 percent. In early 2022, California's GDP was over $3.3 trillion, but some experts estimate its unfunded pension liability at nearly a trillion dollars or $80,000 per state taxpayer.

California has a flat corporate income tax rate of 8.84 percent of gross income. Meanwhile, Texas has no state corporate income tax. It didn't help that in California, businesses had to shut down and were crippled because of COVID-19 restrictions. Many small businesses, a larger percentage of which were owned by minorities, closed their doors forever. California, traditionally one of the major tourist destinations in the nation, saw a steep decline in tourism.

These are cold, hard facts, and they demand real leadership to make improvements. But when I look at Newsom, I shudder. The fact that he has presidential ambitions only makes it worse. This, after all, is a man who is more radical than Bernie Sanders.

Consider: In 2021, Newsom set up a task force on reparations that recommended a $233,000 payment per person for black Californians who are descendants of slaves. This would come to half a trillion dollars. He mandates that every high school student take a course in "ethnic studies." He signed a bill forcing large toy stores to have a "gender neutral" aisle. He opposes sentencing enhancements for criminal gang members because gangs in California are disproportionately black and brown and therefore to punish them commensurate with the severity of their crimes would be "systemic racism." To fight "climate change," he banned the sale of gas-powered lawn mowers and leaf blowers and has outlawed the sale of new gas-powered cars by 2035. He signed a bill mandating that every publicly held corporation headquartered in California have at least one member of a "disadvantaged" group on its board of directors. He signed a bill establishing a council to set the wages of fast-food workers with a minimum hourly rate, effective this year, of twenty-two dollars per hour, a 47 percent increase compared to the previous year.

To deal with COVID-19 in 2020 (and long afterward), he shut down the state—including business, schools, and churches—in a more severe way than any other state and made it mandatory that all state workers be vaccinated or tested regularly and wear masks at work. He expanded taxpayer healthcare for illegal aliens. Under Newsom, California is a sanctuary state for illegal aliens, and jails have been discouraged from referring criminal illegal aliens to ICE, which might deport them.

Newsom offers taxpayer funds to make California a sanctuary state for out-of-staters who come to California for abortions. He supported Proposition 1, approved by voters, that allows abortion up until the point of birth. He endorsed the candidacy of San Francisco DA Chesa Boudin, who was recalled by the city's voters in 2022 because of his soft-on-crime policies. Newsom supported Proposition 47 that allows shoplifters who steal $950 or less to face only misdemeanor charges and, with the help of cashless bail, face no prospect of going to jail. Newsom supported Proposition 57 that redefined many categories of crime as "nonviolent," including assault on a police officer, serial arson, felony domestic violence, and rape of an intoxicated victim.

Newsom has approved a series of tax hikes that, among other decisions demonstrating fiscal irresponsibility, earned him a D in the libertarian CATO Institute's biennial report card for the nation's governors. When he was two-term mayor of San Francisco, homelessness increased in the city, even though he promised to end it by the time he left office, and homelessness has surged in the *state* since he's been governor.

While spending more on education per capita than ever, California schools rank near the bottom of all fifty states. Newsom opposes school choice because teachers unions support him financially, while his own kids attend private school.

Under Newsom, California is losing population for the first time in the state's 170-year history. Meanwhile, the state faces a projected $24 billion deficit.

And this is only a partial list!

At the same time, as I mull this failure of Democratic governance, I have been traveling to Iowa a lot recently. In the summer of last year, I was at the Iowa State Fair when someone came up to me.

"Are you Larry Elder? Why on earth are you here?" she asked.

"I'm here for a pork chop on a stick," I joked.

She laughed too, but then I leveled with her and told her that I was thinking about running for office. She folded her arms and gave me that look that meant I had some explaining to do.

"What's your pitch?" she asked. "I mean, honestly, how would you explain your run to a regular person?"

I was impressed. But then again, people in Iowa are used to asking these blunt questions. I told her that, of course, there are the obvious issues on which all Republicans focus: the economy, inflation, energy independence, and so many others Republicans have been hammering away on for the last two decades.

"But I bring something else to the table that I don't think anyone else is talking about," I told her. "I'm here because I want Republicans to recognize the importance of the nuclear family, intact, especially in black households."

This is a message that I think contributes to the whole of the country. We need to step up our game. Look at Olympics basketball, for example. We used to be able to beat the crap out of the rest of the world. But in the past few decades, they've gotten better than us. They didn't do that by lowering the hoop. They worked harder. Now we have to fight to win at the Olympics. We need to raise our game. We need to get better.

This is why it matters so much that we truly value families and schools. Eighty-five percent of our black eighth graders are neither math- nor reading-proficient. Half of them aren't considered to be proficient, even on a basic level. So a large number of black kids are functionally illiterate and cannot do math.

This is a scandal of epic proportions, and, in my opinion, our side doesn't talk about it enough. The Left is willing to give lip service to the problem—now and then. Barack Obama once gave a speech on Father's Day and talked about the importance of the father. He pointed out that a kid without a father is five times more likely to be poor and commit crime and nine times more likely to drop out of school and likely to end up in jail. It's great that he said that, but under his leadership and his party's governance, we went from having 25 percent of black kids born outside of wedlock in 1965 to 70 percent now, when America is clearly more prosperous and objectively less racist than it was in 1965.

Our side—the GOP—does not question these facts often enough, although the answer is right before our eyes.

I would submit that this is a result of the welfare state. Since 1964, when Lyndon Johnson launched the so-called War on Poverty, we've spent probably over $22 trillion, and it's induced a higher dependency. I've said many times that the welfare state has incentivized women to effectively marry the government while incentivizing men to abandon their financial and moral responsibilities. There was a booklet published in 1965 called *The Negro Family: A Case for National Action*, written by Senator Daniel Patrick Moynihan. At the time, he said 20.5 percent of black kids were born outside of wedlock, which he thought was a growing, festering scandal. He attributed it to the effects of slavery and Jim Crow.

You can debate whether that's true or false, but clearly, you can't attribute the subsequent increase to 70 percent to slavery and Jim Crow. So something happened between 1965 and 1970. Now, 25 percent of white kids come into the world without a father married to the mother, half of Hispanic kids, and 40 percent of all American kids. And we are ignoring that. We talk about the symptoms, sure, but never the source. It's crucial that we do. Besides, growing up in a broken family is not a death sentence. My father never knew his biological father, and he got out. But only through hard, hard work.

Hard work is not something either party really wants to talk about these days, especially when the matter is tinged with race. Republicans avoid the subject altogether—for fear of being called racist—and Democrats condescend to blacks with suggestions such as reparations, one of the most absurd political fads of the last two decades. Even Barack Obama, who so frequently turned his back on reason, pointed out that reparations are completely unworkable, even on a practical level, in 2016: "It is hard to think of any society in human history in which a majority population has said that as a consequence of historic wrongs, we are now going to take a big chunk of the nation's resources over a long period of time to make that right," he told the essayist Ta-Nehisi Coates. "So the bottom line is that it's hard to find a model in which you can practically administer and sustain political support for those kinds of efforts."[67]

Just 26 percent of Americans support reparations, and fewer than 5 percent of whites in America have a "generational" tie to slavery, but that doesn't stop reparations proponents, who often say things like "slavery built America" or "America was built on the backs of slaves." If American taxpayers pay reparations, can they also sue Africa for its role in selling captured and enslaved Africans to Arab and European slavers? What about Native Americans? Have they received sufficient reparations? Or what about the more than three hundred and fifty thousand Union soldiers who died, with another two hundred and fifty thousand who suffered injuries, in the Civil War? Should their descendants pay reparations to the descendants of the slaves their ancestors died to free? It's a nonsensical idea all the way down, and it sidesteps the real issues.

Not only are reparations nonsensical, they are part and parcel with a series of ideologies that converged in real political violence in the summer of 2020 when the Black Lives Matter riots unleashed a wave of crime that resulted in the deaths of at least twenty-five people, thousands of arrests, the injury of two thousand cops, and, according to Axios, "at least $1 billion to $2 billion of paid insurance claims." *RealClearInvestigations* concluded "the 2020 BLM riots resulted in 15 times more injured police officers, 30 times as many arrests, and estimated

67 Ta-Nehisi Coates, "'Better Is Good': Obama on Reparations, Civil Rights, and the Art of the Possible," *The Atlantic*, December 21, 2016, https://www.theatlantic.com/politics/archive/2016/12/ta-nehisi-coates-obama-transcript.

damages in dollar terms up to 1,300 times more costly than those of the Capitol riot."

Let's recall the facts. In May of 2020, George Floyd's tragic death triggered weeks of sustained chaos in America. Democratic mayors and "woke" DAs stepped aside and let mobs ransack our cities in the name of "racial justice." The results were catastrophic, both for the country and for black people.

In the aftermath of the riots, murders increased by an astounding 29.4 percent nationwide, according to the FBI. In Minnesota, murders rose by 58 percent. In Denver, killings went up by 50 percent. In Chicago, by 55 percent. And in New York City, by 44 percent. In Los Angeles, where I live, murder hit a fifteen-year high in 2021 and is, as of this writing, is on pace to eclipse that 2022 mark.

And who is it that receives the brunt of this violence? Who is being killed in the streets? For the most part, it's black people. While our cities burned in 2020, numerous Democratic Party officials were given the chance to tell rioters to stand down. Astoundingly, many chose to do the opposite.

We need to make sure that this never happens again. We need to understand why, in the midst of the largest domestic terrorism event of our lives, so many Democratic officials stood aside—or in some cases, give cover to the rioters? Were politicians like Vice President Harris merely dog-whistling their support for political violence? Was it just incompetence that caused leaders like Gavin Newsom to be asleep at the switch? Was there wider collusion between senior Democrats in Washington and local officials to use this insurrection for political gain?

Democrats like Joe Biden and Nancy Pelosi like to say that they want to fight "systemic racism" and strive for "racial equality." But the wave of crime their policies have unleashed has done the opposite.

I submit that the solution to all these issues is pretty simple—and has nothing to do with racism. If there's one policy proposal I would make as president, it would be to fix the schools and make sure that every American, black, white, Asian—whatever—can get a good education.

If I become president, here's what I would do on my first day in office.

I would give a speech about the promise of America, the kinds of things that I believe Barack Obama was elected to do and failed to do. Obama was such a disappointment, to black people especially. He was well-educated and accomplished, and he still believes that America is systemically racist. Worse, he wasn't Al Sharpton. He wasn't Jesse Jackson. He's a smooth, polished guy who went to Punahou, Occidental, Columbia, and Harvard. That's why he was elected. He was elected to show America the opposite of systemic racism, yet he reinforced all this white supremacy tropes, and that made him even more dangerous, because he was more persuasive and articulate than the race hustlers who preceded him.

If elected, I would be the black president America thought they were electing with Barack Obama. Of course, unlike Obama, I would support lower taxes, less regulations, securing the borders, and getting us back to energy independence—everything other Republicans have been advocating for decades.

I do not make the decision to run lightly. In fact, as I weighed my chances, I went back and consulted the same people who urged me to run in California. The responses were overwhelmingly enthusiastic.

Ginny Sand, who fought so hard to convince me to run for governor, made a similar case for me to throw my hat in the ring for the presidency.

"Larry has an enormous sense of gratitude—for the values instilled in him by his parents, the sacrifices his forebears made, and the opportunities offered to him by the greatest country in the history of the world," she said. "He knows how much he owes them and has a tremendous desire to give back, to make a difference, and to live up to his mother's dreams for him."

She added that my reasons for running are serious and personal—true equality through universal school choice—and that I have a message that every educational establishment needs to teach. Educators need to reject the accepted lie that this country is systemically racist. The real struggle that blacks are facing today, from the moment they are born, is the tragic, government-caused breakdown of the family and absence of fathers in the home. That's something I've been saying for years, and Ginny pointed out that it needs to be said on the national stage.

Pastor Jack Hibbs told me that I had run my gubernatorial campaign with integrity, courage, and a vision for California that could have positively impacted and transformed California for several generations. And, he added, wherever I go, I would make a great political leader—and president.

Dennis Prager was also enthusiastic. Those same four traits that he said would serve me so well running against

Newsom—courage and truthfulness, as well as the fact I didn't seek to be loved, and my outsider status—would also help me on the national stage.

"Larry possesses all four traits of a great person," Dennis said, "We'll begin with courage. It takes a great deal of courage for a black public figure to criticize black leaders and defend America against charges of racism. I witnessed firsthand the intense hatred directed at Larry almost from the moment he began his radio career—including boycotts of his radio show and of the companies that advertised on it. Yet he never compromised.

"He never compromised because of his unwavering commitment to telling the truth. Larry can no more lie than a lion can turn into a mouse. He seems incapable of saying anything he does not believe to be true.

"Because of his courage, his commitment to finding and only telling the truth, and not seeking to be loved (though he is deeply loved by many), Larry is the quintessential outlier.

"America needs great men now more than at any time since Abraham Lincoln. Thank God, Larry is not the only great American, but there are not many who run for public office. That one of them seeks the presidency provides more than a ray of light in a very dark time.

"Knowing Larry as well as I do, I can't wait to see and hear him on the stage in the Republican primary debates. Americans won't know what hit them."

I hope I can live up to such high praise.

And, as I survey the potential 2024 field, I see much hope for our country. Take Florida governor Ron DeSantis. He's a rock star. What he did in challenging the orthodoxy on COVID-19?

That took cashews and could have gone the wrong way. Ditto for taking on Disney. He's bright, he's got a beautiful wife, and he's a military man. He connects all the dots.

I'm also impressed with Glenn Youngkin who, from what I've seen so far, is doing great work in Virginia. In Iowa, Kim Reynolds—who is unjustly overlooked—is doing a great job. She won her most recent race by a wide margin in a year Republicans swept the state. She's lowered taxes across the board. I've spoken with her a lot, and I have great respect for her.

Of course, I couldn't mention all these wonderful potential candidates without talking about Donald Trump. When you look at his presidency, he accomplished more in four years than most Republicans have in a half a century. Under his leadership, America boomed. The country became oil and gas self-sufficient. He secured the borders—making it less porous, border agents said, than at any time in memory. Black Americans prospered. The US recorded the lowest unemployment rate for blacks in history. Forty-five percent of minority and black-owned small businesses grew by 400 percent. The First Step Act was unparalleled criminal justice reform, allowing over five thousand mostly black prisoners to have their sentences reconsidered and reduced by an average of seventy months. Trump signed the FUTURE Act, allocating funding on a permanent basis beyond 2019 for Historically Black Colleges and Universities. He expanded Opportunity Zones and provided capital gains tax breaks for those who invest in low-income census tracts.

Trump pardoned Jack Johnson, the first black heavyweight champion, found guilty and jailed for violating the